Focus

"For CEOs strategy planning can be frustrating. Finally, a clean approach that can focus and sequence the work, bring the voice of the customer to the center of the plan, provide a concrete link between strategy and sales growth, and mitigate analysis paralysis."

—John Kaul, Chief Executive Officer, *Allredi*

"If you want to build a business strategy that drives financial outcomes like sales, revenue & profitability, stop using your current approach. Customer-based strategy is the only framework that links customer value to product portfolio & customer segmentation choices, investment & budgeting decisions, aligned priorities for all departments, and individual accountability & performance."

—Maggie Seeliger, *Senior Vice President—Strategy, Sodexo Energy and Resources Worldwide*

"I've been involved in strategy planning for numerous organizations. This book's approach is a quantum leap forward. It focuses, streamlines, and improves strategy planning bringing customer value at the center of it."

—Heather Wisialowski, Chief Revenue Officer, *Allredi*

"Implementing this strategy approach cut out all the guess work from strategy planning work. As the CEO, I can finally link strategy to financial outcomes, prioritize initiatives, and focus my senior executives on what matters most to our clients."

—Simon Seaton, Chief Executive Officer, *Sodexo Energy and Resources Worldwide*

"Boards, CEOs, and senior executives use a lot of gut feel and guesswork in strategy planning. This book first documents why that can harm strategy planning and then shows how a modern approach rooted in scientific thinking can reform the strategy process. As the CEO of many successful companies, I highly recommend this book to those aspiring to be transformative CEOs and strategy leaders."

—Rahul Mehta, Chief Executive Officer, *Mehta Family Foundation and NuView, Inc.*

Vikas Mittal • Shrihari Sridhar

Focus

How to Plan Strategy and Improve Execution to Achieve Growth

Vikas Mittal
Rice University
Houston, TX, USA

Shrihari Sridhar
Texas A&M University
College Station, TX, USA

ISBN 978-3-030-70719-4   ISBN 978-3-030-70720-0   (eBook)
https://doi.org/10.1007/978-3-030-70720-0

This Palgrave Macmillan imprint is published by the registered company Springer Nature Switzerland AG.
The registered company address is: Gewerbestrasse 11, 6330 Cham, Switzerland

Preface

Shrihari Sridhar CEOs and senior executives have exciting and invigorating jobs. They are charged with formulating a strategy to focus and align their organization to deliver sales and profit growth. They are also responsible for executing the strategy to the satisfaction of their board with the help of many stakeholders, including employees and suppliers. In theory, senior executives should view their charge as one of the most exciting opportunities to impact their organization.

Executives' jobs are also mind-bogglingly frustrating. On an ongoing basis, senior executives develop their company's mission and vision, finalize its budget, manage stakeholder expectations, execute strategy, assess ongoing risks, fight fires, and communicate with the outside world. Their efforts occur against an industry backdrop in which they not only have less autonomy and shorter tenure than two decades ago, but they also must deal with heightened demands for accountability, transparency, and scrutiny. They must reckon with increasingly rapid technological change and intense competition. It is not surprising many executives feel worn out by strategy and execution.

According to CEOs, the biggest issue confronting executives is the need for perennial and sustained focus. CEOs need ways to focus their senior executives' efforts in developing and executing coherent strategy, a challenge heightened by the divergent goals and demands of diverse stakeholders—customers, employees, suppliers, shareholders, and board members. As one CEO stated:

> The board wants me to cut costs and grow margins, institutional investors want me to promote a sustainability agenda, employees are frustrated with layoffs. Customers seek better after-sales service. I've taken out over a billion dollars in costs, but the strategy has left most customers and employees unsatisfied.

Another CEO said of creating strategy for an energy company:

> I hear from the sales team that safety is the key differentiator for winning new work, even though every interaction with clients reveals that our bids are over-priced. To this, the board constantly reminds me that we have not fulfilled our strategy goal of being fully digital by 2020, and this has irked some institutional shareholders who questioned the company's lackluster CSR score in the last investor call.

This book addresses four questions asked by many CEOs:

- What is the state of strategy formulation and execution in companies like mine?
- Why is the strategy process so frustrating and difficult, and how can it be simplified?
- How can senior executives on my team meaningfully improve strategy planning and execution to grow sales and profit?
- How can my company hold the strategy planning process to account?

To test whether executives understand the four questions' nuances, this book asks them to take a simple quiz consisting of ten questions. The resulting scores provide a strategy planning quotient, a realistic read of respondents' understanding of the strategy process based on research, rather than hearsay. Most executives' quotients are far lower than they expect, a stark reminder of why this book can help them achieve extraordinary results through strategy planning and execution.

Our research over a four-year period includes multiple large-scale assessments of more than 6000 executives and managers in varied industries, surveys of over 11,000 customers of different companies, a systematic meta-analysis of strategy outcomes research over the past 70 years, more than 100 hours of in-depth interviews and discussions with senior executives and CEOs, and a series of workshops with board members and executives to test and refine our ideas. This book's overarching theme—a need for systematic focus—surfaced again and again throughout the research process.

CEOs value strategy planning but see it as a complex process that could be dramatically improved. In-depth interviews uncovered eight central issues that beset strategy planning processes and frustrate CEOs. The issues affect companies' broad direction and extend to concrete strategy implementation by senior executives and middle management. CEOs and senior executives who read this book will relate to the eight frustrations, but they will also learn to alleviate them through a strategy process engaging leadership more meaningfully, better leveraging their ideas, and coordinating their actions for superior results.

To validate the executives' views, this book compiles and examines a broad set of evidence. We surveyed thousands of employees, managers and executives, and customers. We examined academic studies published in peer-reviewed journals, systematic reviews and meta-analyses of published empirical research, and in-depth business case studies. The research consistently showed

employees were skeptical
ent most of their time on
lanning had no association
ded with a large-scale syn-
itegy planning correlations
ig has little to no statistical
r executives are wary of its

of strategy planning? The
to strategy planning—the
aches. Companies typically
use some combination of the three. Each approach brings its own assumptions, constraints, and inhibitors, which impede well-meaning executives' realization of their strategy plan's promise. To delve deeper into the strategy planning approaches, the book deconstructs their efficacy using a combination of in-depth interviews, synthesis of more than five decades of academic studies, and our own original research.

The inspirational strategy planning approach is rooted in anthropology and predicated on senior executives' ability to articulate their organization's mission, vision, and values. The mission, vision, and values motivate senior and middle management and frontline employees to follow their company's north star. Notwithstanding its purported advantages, the approach (1) tends to be subjective and vague; (2) has an overly broad and overarching scope; (3) is inward looking, echoing senior executives' desires but eschewing customer needs; and (4) rarely provides the focus and clarity employees need to implement strategy. New research shared in this book shows mission statements serve senior leaders' aspirations and de-emphasize strategy areas important to customers. And virtually no statistical association emerges between elements of company mission statements and customer needs.

The adhocratic approach to strategy planning is informal, unstructured, and emergent, and embraces experimentation and improvisation. Typically used in startups and small businesses, the approach relies on routine, day-to-day implementation activities to provide a stable, consistent, and repeatable framework for identifying and meeting strategy goals. Multiple peer-reviewed studies show adhocracies foster unending experimentation and improvisation at the expense of predictability through repeatable and stable systems. Our research shows adhocratic strategy planning processes heavily favor innovation, technology, product development, flexibility, and adaptability. The approach fosters an internal focus, tilting companies away from customers. Indeed, adhocratic companies satisfy only 2%–6% of their customers' needs.

The budget-based strategy planning approach, rooted in economics, finance, and operations management, emphasizes formal and systematic processes to couple budgeting with goal setting, resource allocation, and employee accountability. Senior executives use budgets to focus on operational excellence and control. Yet, research shows elaborate budget-based plans serve more as signals to external stakeholders than coherent strategies. Our research shows budget-based strategy makes companies inward looking instead of customer focused, which inevitably hurts performance.

Why should one read this book? Board members, CEOs, senior executives, middle managers, and C-suite aspirants will gain a deep understanding of the three strategy planning approaches and their potential pitfalls when it comes to delivering financial results. The book uncovers seven strategy planning inhibitors that impede the process's effectiveness in companies large and small. The inhibitors do not reflect executives' inherent weaknesses. Nor can executives eliminate the inhibitors by being aware of their existence or being more thoughtful. Strategy inhibitors are behavioral tendencies impeding the planning process, and systematic changes are required to eliminate them.

This book delineates seven research-based strategy enablers executives can use to un-inhibit their inhibitors. The enablers go beyond the usual prescriptions and exhortations for senior executives to be smarter, better problem solvers, and more thoughtful. They serve as systematic factors that must be incorporated in the strategy process at all levels: Replacing salience-based decisions with a scientifically developed strategy map, developing consensus on the map's components, developing measures of strategy components and weighting them based on importance, using mathematical analysis to calculate the give-get weights of each strategy map linkage, and setting aside one's ego, personal biases, and salient thoughts to accept the strategy analysis.

The book closes with the story of Exterior, Inc., a premium-price manufacturer of roofing tiles for custom-home builders. Exterior's CEO, working diligently with his senior executives, transformed the company's strategy process and goals and achieved financial success through three phases: a strategy dilemma, a shift to customer-focused strategy formulation, and committing to customer-focused strategy implementation. The story illustrates the difficulties of strategy planning, common CEO frustrations, and potential strategy inhibitors and enablers. It serves as a powerful reminder that implementing an enabled strategy process requires complete and unwavering commitment from the entire senior executive team.

For C-suite executives (e.g., chief executive officers, chief financial officers, and chief strategy officers), senior executives (e.g., vice presidents, senior vice presidents, and division presidents), middle managers (e.g., directors and senior managers) and others aspiring to leadership positions, functional executives (e.g., sales, marketing, supply chain, and operations directors) seeking corporate roles, and management students, this book provides a robust strategy planning framework consisting of five repeatable and predictable milestones. It should appeal to board members wanting to eliminate inhibitors and inculcate enablers for budding CEOs.

Many change management consultants seek specific examples, frameworks, and toolkits to help senior executives change their strategy process. Yet, most available material focuses on personal change management and executive self-improvement. This book takes the opposite perspective. To enhance its strategy formulation, a company doesn't have to make its executives smarter or better. By identifying inhibitors and replacing them with enablers, companies can allow ordinary CEOs and executives to achieve extraordinary results.

We invite you to read this book and embark on your transformational journey—to transform the strategy process in your organization. Start by taking the quiz in Chap. 1 to calculate your strategy planning quotient, a measure of your understanding of strategy planning. We challenge you to improve it!

Houston, TX

Vikas Mittal
Shrihari Sridhar

Acknowledgments

We have many people to thank for this book's beautiful four-year journey. Vikas thanks his wife, Nandita Gupta, and daughter, Sukul Mittal, for enabling him in more ways than they can imagine. Shrihari (Hari) thanks his wife, Akshaya Sreenivasan, and son, Virat Shrihari, who are the very purpose of his existence and for all things positive and worth appreciating in life.

Beyond our families, so many people have contributed to making this endeavor fulfilling. We are grateful to the many co-authors and doctoral students who have provided unwavering commitment and support to our research over the years. Shea Gibbs at Gibbs Communications has been an invaluable ally throughout this journey. We thank all our undergraduate, MBA, MS analytics, and executive students, whose questions and suggestions have taught us new ways to look at the age-old problem of strategy planning.

This book would not be possible without the fidelity and commitment of dozens of CEOs and senior executives, who showed the flexibility necessary to think differently in pursuit of their transformative strategy. Terry Grier, John Kaul, Joshua Robinson, Simon Seaton, Maggie Seeliger, and Heather Wisialowski generously shared their time and perspective, provided input, and listened to and critiqued ideas different from their own. Bo Bothe, Jonathan Fisher, Bonnie Houston, and Ravi Kathuria shared their perspective and frustrations on strategy implementation and provided feedback on earlier drafts of our work. Paul DeLisi, Troy Thacker, and Alan

Ying provided strategy planning perspectives from the private equity vantage point, underscoring the crucial role of senior executives in strategy planning and execution.

Finally, we cannot adequately express our gratitude to Rahul Mehta—our Yoda, personal mentor, and motivator. Rahul has consistently believed in us, the ideas expressed in this book, and this endeavor's potential more than even we ourselves have.

Contents

1 Strategy Planning in the Real World   1
   1.1   Understanding Strategy Planning   1
   1.2   Eight Strategy Stories   2
   1.3   Calculating Your Strategy Planning Quotient   4
   1.4   Improving Your Strategy Planning Quotient   8

2 The CEO Perspective on Strategy Planning   11
   2.1   Listening to CEOs   12
   2.2   One: Lacking a Customer Lens   13
   2.3   Two: Informed by Siloed and Bifurcated Research That Misleads   14
   2.4   Three: No Meaningful Comparisons   16
   2.5   Four: Analysis Paralysis   17
   2.6   Five: Lacking a Link Between Strategy and Financial Outcomes   18
   2.7   Six: No Meaningful Way to Focus and Sequence Executives' Effort   20
   2.8   Seven: Following Executives' Personal Preferences to Define Strategy   21
   2.9   Eight: No Blueprint for Alignment   23
   2.10   Conclusion   24

3 The Perils and Promise of Strategy Planning   25
   3.1   What CEOs Believe   25
   3.2   What Senior Executives and Managers Believe   26
   3.3   Executives' Subjective Beliefs and Objective Reality   29

3.4   Three Studies of Executive Beliefs   35
3.5   National Study of Executive Beliefs   40
3.6   FACILITYCO Executives' Beliefs and Customer Needs   41
3.7   Mitigating Perils and Maximizing Promise   43

**4   The Inspirational Executive: Strategy Planning Through
Mission, Vision, and Values**   47
4.1   Understanding the Inspirational Approach   48
4.2   Evaluating the Inspirational Approach to Strategy   53
4.3   The Perils of Mission Statements   55
4.4   The Inspirational Approach: Research Evidence   56
4.5   Conclusion   61

**5   The Superhero Executive: Strategy Planning Through
Adhocracy**   65
5.1   Overemphasizing Exploration   68
5.2   Overemphasizing Innovation   71
5.3   Pioneering Industries   72
5.4   New Research   73
5.5   Conclusion   77

6   The Analytical Executive: Budget-Based Strategy Planning   81
6.1   Evaluating the Budget-Based Approach   84
6.2   Examining New Evidence   91
6.3   Conclusion   96

7   Strategy Planning Inhibitors   99
7.1   Inhibitor 1: Confusing Salience with Importance   100
7.2   Inhibitor 2: Intuitive Leaps   103
7.3   Inhibitor 3: Belief in Mythical Numbers   108
7.4   Inhibitor 4: Staying Put   110
7.5   Inhibitor 5: More-Is-Better Thinking   114
7.6   Inhibitor 6: Inwardly Focused and Discordant   115
7.7   Inhibitor 7: Decoupled Measurement and Diffuse
Accountability   119
7.8   Conclusion   121

8   Strategy Planning Enablers   127
8.1   Enabler 1: Chain-link Your Strategy Map   129
8.2   Enabler 2: Know the Give-Get of Each Link   131

8.3	Enabler 3: Achieve More by Doing Less	133
8.4	Enabler 4: Relentlessly Implement the Not-To-Do List	134
8.5	Enabler 5: Flip the Planning Template	136
8.6	Enabler 6: Embed Science in Strategy Planning	137
8.7	Enabler 7: Approach the Planning Process with Humility	139
8.8	Conclusion	140

9   Exterior, Inc.'s Strategy Success Story   143
9.1	Exterior, Inc.: 2008–2014	144
9.2	Exterior's Strategy Planning Dilemma: 2014	145
9.3	Rewiring the Strategy Planning Process: 2015	149
9.4	Exterior's Strategy Enabled Not Inhibited: 2015–2017	153
9.5	Conclusion	157

10   Increasing the Strategy Planning Quotient   159
10.1	Not All CEOs Are Strategy Leaders	160
10.2	How Can CEOs Increase Their Strategy Planning Quotient?	163
10.3	How Can Senior Executives Increase Their Strategy Planning Quotient?	165
10.4	Review and Refine Your Company's Strategy Process	167
10.5	Creating a Robust Strategy Planning Framework	169
10.6	Conclusion	171

Index   173

List of Figures

Fig. 1.1 Strategy planning quotient scoring sheet 8
Fig. 2.1 CEOs' issues with strategy planning 13
Fig. 3.1 Executives' agreement with CEOs' top-three strategy objectives 28
Fig. 3.2 Time executives spend on activities/areas 29
Fig. 3.3 Association between strategy planning and performance outcomes 33
Fig. 3.4 Executive MBA student survey's respondent profile 36
Fig. 3.5 Executives' opinions on strategy planning 36
Fig. 3.6 Executives' perception of correlation between strategy goals and sales/profits 37
Fig. 3.7 Executives' perceived impact of strategy planning 38
Fig. 3.8 Advisory group's beliefs about strategy planning and sales/profits 39
Fig. 3.9 Survey of energy industry advisory group 39
Fig. 4.1 Comparing strategic areas for energy companies using mission statements 57
Fig. 4.2 Comparing strategic areas for energy companies using 10-K reports 58
Fig. 4.3 Comparing strategic areas for B2B companies using mission statements 60
Fig. 4.4 Comparing strategic areas for B2B companies using 10-K reports 60
Fig. 5.1 How eight strategic areas drive B2B customer value 74
Fig. 5.2 How execution levers enhance product/service quality for B2B customers 75
Fig. 5.3 How eight strategic areas drive value for energy customers 76
Fig. 5.4 How execution levers enhance product/service quality for energy customers 76

Fig. 6.1   Customer satisfaction, efficiency, and gross margin   95
Fig. 6.2   Comparison of relative satisfaction with strategic areas   96
Fig. 7.1   Strategic area salience and importance for FOODCO   101
Fig. 7.2   Intuitive leaps at nursing homes   104
Fig. 7.3   Intuitive leaps at FOODCO   106
Fig. 7.4   Decoupled metrics at SCHOOLCO   121
Fig. 10.1   Strategy process milestones   170

List of Tables

Table 3.1   Strategy planning effectiveness by measure type   33
Table 3.2   Strategy planning effectiveness incidence by measure type   35
Table 3.3   Misalignment of FACILITYCO executives and customers   42
Table 6.1   Importance of product/service in driving customer value   92
Table 6.2   Financial performance and perceived product quality   93
Table 9.1   Exterior Inc.'s performance, 2007 versus 2014   145
Table 9.2   Customer assessment results, 2015   151
Table 9.3   Customer assessment results, 2015   153
Table 9.4   Customer assessment results, 2017   157

1

Strategy Planning in the Real World

1.1   Understanding Strategy Planning

Strategy planning is the process by which a company sets goals, assigns resources, defines major initiatives, and creates a budget. It is a critical activity for most of the corporate world. More than 88% of all large companies engage in a formal strategy planning process at regular intervals, ranging from one year to ten years.[1]

Oil and gas companies like Shell, Texaco, and Elf have reported using dual systems that include medium- and long-term strategic plans spanning 5–10 years.[2] But strategy planning is not restricted to large companies. More than 80% of small- and medium-sized firms have formal strategy plans that they update at one- to three-year intervals.[3]

Strategy planning varies across companies. Some admit to using an intuitive and emergent approach. Other companies use strategy planning to define, refine, or emphasize their mission, vision, and values. Others create formal plans integrating financial budgeting and operational planning; the strategy sets the financial and operational priorities for the upcoming plan period. Companies like Amoco and ExxonMobil use strategy plans emphasizing broad strategic themes, such as becoming a global gas business with a cost-reduction focus, but do not specify formal action plans.[4]

Why is strategy planning important? Given unpredictable future events, marketplace turbulence, intense competitive pressure, evolving customer needs, and ever-changing technology, regulations, and societies, executives use strategy planning to see the big picture. In an ideal world, strategy plans

© The Author(s), under exclusive license to Springer Nature Switzerland AG 2021
V. Mittal, S. Sridhar, *Focus*, https://doi.org/10.1007/978-3-030-70720-0_1

help a company identify its top priorities, align resources to priorities, and use the resources to drive accountability at all organizational levels.

How does strategy planning unfold at different companies, and does it help senior executives achieve their goals? Whether through corporate retreats or deep-dive sessions, small and large companies discuss viewpoints, debate alternative strategies, develop mission statements, create goals, and use execution plans to implement and achieve their goals.

1.2   Eight Strategy Stories

CEOs and senior executives face many situations—simple to complex, sad to funny, perplexing to straightforward—during strategy planning. In the following strategy planning stories, the names of the companies have been changed to maintain their anonymity.

Engineering and Projects Company (EPCO). EPCO is a major engineering and procurement company headquartered in Houston, with sales offices in the Middle East, South America, North America, and Asia. Due to EPCO's declining business, the executive team convinced the CEO to tilt the company's strategy plan toward acquiring new customers. With a project win rate of 28%, the team reasoned that a larger pipeline of bids would translate to more sales. The chief sales officer commented, "This will allow us to forge a new direction to turn the company around."

As the company bid more, its win rate did not improve, nor did its backlog. Customers started complaining about poorly managed projects, missed deadlines, and lack of communication among project staff. With several cancelled projects, the CEO eventually reorganized the company, replacing all but two senior executives.

Fast Casual Restaurant Chain (FOODCO). When the lunch-focused restaurant chain FOODCO was hit with stagnating sales, its CEO and owner wanted to improve its strategy. He focused on the many different menu items he believed would preserve FOODCO's "high quality"—freshly prepared sandwiches, soups, and salads. Yet, customer surveys showed that customers wanted a fast dining experience with a short wait time, a simple menu with few items, ample parking, and a bill lower than $12 per meal, drinks included. The survey results contrasted starkly with the strategy direction FOODCO's owner charted.

When FOODCO's owner read the survey findings, he said, "This validates what has been clear to me all along. We have to lead and not be led. Too often, customers don't know what they want, and we have to shape their needs.

Look at Apple. We need a winning strategy that differentiates our brands, and we can do that by offering the largest selection of freshly prepared foods at the lowest price point in the marketplace."

Machine Tools Solutions Company (TOOLCO). TOOLCO's project management division included 80 people: 10 senior leaders, 26 project directors, and 44 analysts, line managers, and support staff. Every year, the division managed more than 200 projects worth $800 million. Division employees spent almost 80% of their time fulfilling projects. They spent their remaining time advancing strategic initiatives related to project management. The division deployed 97 strategic initiatives, of which only nine were deemed effective.

During a strategy retreat, TOOLCO's senior executives reviewed the initiatives. They decided to add two initiatives to increase the effectiveness of their current portfolio of initiatives. One initiative was to create a 360-degree view of the project management process through an expensive CRM system. A second initiative was to add more quality control training modules. The managers prepared a proposal to increase TOOLCO's annual strategy implementation budget from $31 million to $40 million.

U.S. Urban School District (SCHOOLCO). At SCHOOLCO, a large K-12 school district and one of the largest nonprofit enterprises in the county, the assistant superintendent for each function—academics, human resources, operations, etc.—contributed to initiatives he or she deemed important. Each assistant superintendent sought to obtain funding, increase staff size, and gain influence and power within the district. SCHOOLCO's strategic plan promised to implement 168 initiatives over five years. Each year, the district added initiatives during the strategy planning process but rarely if ever removed initiatives.

Onsite-Medical Company (MEDCO). The physician-owner of a medical practice focused on the daily activities while running the firm. MEDCO therefore made strategy decisions, such as upgrading medical-records software, outsourcing billing, and adding new patient segments, on an ad hoc basis. For MEDCO, action was primary, and planning was a support activity. MEDCO's weekly meetings functioned as strategy meetings. "I don't have the luxury that big corporations have," the physician-owner said. "Strategy planning will cost me thousands of dollars in time and money. All I need to do is maintain my daily average of 20 patients, and I'm good to go."

Property Management Company (REALTYCO). The president of a small property management company focused on ensuring all his firm's properties were rented and maintained. While REALTYCO's strategy goal was to grow the number of properties under management, its daily activities were focused on ensuring clients—property owners and renters—were satisfied. The company emphasized process innovations, such as online software for rent deposits, outsourcing accounting, and using social media, to gain customers. REALTYCO's president admitted he did not have a strategy plan or goals. The company decided to set goals to streamline activities and provide employees guidance. REALTYCO's new strategy goals were to increase properties under management from 120 to 170, use technology to lower operational costs, and grow the firm's social media presence to increase following among local renters.

Integrated Facilities Management, Catering, and Support Company (FACILITYCO). FACILITYCO, a subsidiary of a global firm, had more than $1.5 billion in annual sales and served clients at 1600 sites worldwide. Upon taking over, the newly appointed CEO met with his senior executives to understand the company's strategy. The executives said the strategy centered around: (1) increasing sales through lead generation and aggressive bidding, (2) sustainability, and (3) safety. The chief sales officer championed the sales initiative, while the company's global headquarters drove the sustainability initiative. When asked about FACILITYCO's strategy, the executives presented the CEO with the firm's annual budget and a five-year sales forecast predicated on steady margin growth. "Our strategy is to maximize margin growth, which can be achieved by driving sales—hence, our focus on lead generation," the executives said.

Manufacturer and Distributor of Industrial Abrasives (ABCO). A coatings firm, operating under a newly appointed CEO, acquired and merged with a rival. The CEO branded both companies under the ABCO name. Eleven senior executives met with the CEO to review the next steps in ABCO's strategy. Prior to the meeting, the CEO asked each executive to list the strategy's key elements. Sixty-two percent said ABCO's strategy was to increase operational and process efficiency, 68% stated it was to grow ABCO through mergers and acquisitions, and 48% said the strategy was to increase revenues. During the meeting, the CEO revealed that ABCO had never undertaken a strategy planning process and did not have a strategy plan.

1.3   Calculating Your Strategy Planning Quotient

Strategy planning can be a time-intensive, all-encompassing, and important aspect of a CEO's leadership agenda. Including the CEO, all members of the senior executive team should approach strategy planning with passion, putting time, effort, and energy into creating and implementing a plan. They can then use the strategy plan and planning process to drive their company's performance.

An underlying belief among most executives is that they fully understand strategy planning—what it entails and how it helps define and achieve company goals and objectives. In other words, many senior executives believe they have a high strategy planning quotient. And rightfully so. Most senior executives have participated in multiple strategy planning exercises and led or implemented strategy for a division, unit, or company.

To test how well you understand strategy, take the quiz below to compute your strategy planning quotient.[5] It will help you understand your planning beliefs and assumptions. Circle the best answer for each question and use the provided scoring sheet to calculate your strategy planning quotient:

Question 1: To what extent does strategy planning drive a company's financial success as measured by outcomes like increased sales and stock price? In other words, which of the following categories most accurately describes the correlation between strategy planning and financial success?

a) 0.00 to 0.20
b) 0.21 to 0.40
c) 0.41 to 0.60
d) 0.61 to 0.80
e) 0.81 to 1.00

Question 2: What percentage of their time do senior executives spend thinking about ways to improve their company's strategy and strategy plan?

a) 0% to 20%
b) 21% to 40%
c) 41% to 60%
d) 61% to 80%
e) 81% to 100%

Question 3: What percentage of their time do senior executives spend on day-to-day tactical activities, unproductive tasks/meetings, politics/firefighting, and convincing others to listen to their point of view?

a) 0% to 20%
b) 21% to 40%
c) 41% to 60%
d) 61% to 80%
e) 81% to 100%

Question 4: Senior executives should base their companies' strategy plans on the most important customer-value drivers, that is, factors important to their customers. What percentage of senior executives correctly identify the three most important customer-value drivers for their company?

a) 0% to 20%
b) 21% to 40%
c) 41% to 60%
d) 61% to 80%
e) 81% to 100%

Question 5: What percentage of senior executives underestimate the impact of increasing customer value on increasing sales?

a) 0% to 20%
b) 21% to 40%
c) 41% to 60%
d) 61% to 80%
e) 81% to 100%

Question 6: What percentage of senior executives are doubtful about the effectiveness of their company's strategy plan?

a) 0% to 20%
b) 21% to 40%
c) 41% to 60%
d) 61% to 80%
e) 81% to 100%

Question 7: In a typical company, what percentage of senior executives agree with the CEO's top two strategy objectives?

a) 0% to 20%
b) 21% to 40%
c) 41% to 60%
d) 61% to 80%
e) 81% to 100%

Question 8: What percentage of senior executives agree that other senior executives in their company understand the company's strategy objectives?

a) 0% to 20%
b) 21% to 40%
c) 41% to 60%
d) 61% to 80%
e) 81% to 100%

Question 9: What percentage of senior executives agree that their company's strategy plan is aligned with employee needs?

a) 0% to 20%
b) 21% to 40%
c) 41% to 60%
d) 61% to 80%
e) 81% to 100%

Question 10: What is the correlation between a company having a mission statement and its financial success?

a) 0.00 to 0.20
b) 0.21 to 0.40
c) 0.41 to 0.60
d) 0.61 to 0.80
e) 0.81 to 1.00

If you scored above 80, you have an excellent or very good strategy planning quotient. Your beliefs and knowledge about strategy planning are very much in line with the reality of the strategy planning process. This book should enable you to build on your above-average understanding of strategy planning to enhance the benefits of the process (Fig. 1.1).

If you scored between 71 and 80, your beliefs and assumptions about strategy planning only partially correspond with the reality of the strategy planning process. Reading this book will provide you with a realistic glimpse of the strategy planning process and improve your understanding of it. You can use the information to update your beliefs and assumptions about strategy planning and improve your success-rate with the process.

If you scored 70 or below, your beliefs and assumptions about strategy planning are very different from the reality of the strategy planning process.

Strategy Planning Quotient Scoring Sheet

Step 1: Circle the number that matches your response to each question.
Step 2: Add your score from each column to obtain your column subtotals.
Step 3: Add your subtotals to obtain your Strategy Planning Quotient.

Q	Option A	Option B	Option C	Option D	Option E
1	10	5	0	-5	-10
2	10	5	0	-5	-10
3	-5	10	10	0	-10
4	10	5	0	-5	-10
5	-10	-5	0	10	5
6	0	10	10	-5	-10
7	5	10	5	-5	-10
8	-10	-10	0	5	10
9	-10	0	5	10	0
10	10	5	0	-5	-10
Subtotals					

TOTAL (Sum of all Subtotals) Your Strategy Planning Quotient	

Your Strategy Planning Quotient	91 -100	Excellent
	81 -90	Very Good
	71 -80	Average
	61 -70	Below Average
	60 & below	Poor

Fig. 1.1 Strategy planning quotient scoring sheet

Reading this book will help you learn the realities of strategy planning and improve your ability to think about strategy in a realistic way. Building on the information, you can approach the strategy planning process with confidence and improve your team's success rate.

1.4   Improving Your Strategy Planning Quotient

Developing a strategy plan and implementing it is perhaps the most important contribution a CEO makes to a company. Yet, even with the highest level of effort and best intentions, strategy plans fail to deliver in many cases. Executives can improve their chances of success by improving their strategy planning quotient.

The first goal of this book is to help students of strategy planning—research scholars, senior executives, aspiring executives, and business students—improve their strategy planning quotient using direct inputs from CEOs and 70-plus years of research. The book incorporates research from statistics and quantitative analysis, psychology, social psychology, organizational behavior, and decision-making to provide an in-depth understanding of the historical roots and progression of the corporate strategy-making process. A deeper understanding of the process, the number of companies that engage in it, and the embedded assumptions executives bring to it are critical. Does a company use budget-based planning or rely on mission/vision statements? What are the costs and benefits of each approach?

The second goal of the book is to help readers appreciate the faulty premises and assumptions that many senior executives bring to the strategy planning process. Many executives base their planning and execution on factors that are salient but not important, make intuitive leaps, use their beliefs about mythical numbers in budgeting, indulge in more-is-better thinking, become inwardly focused and discordant, decouple measurement, and diffuse responsibility.

The book's third goal is to help readers appreciate that simply knowing strategic inhibitors is not enough to change and improve a company's strategy process. Executives must replace the inhibitors with the appropriate enablers, which requires incorporating statistical analysis to chain-link a company's strategy and quantify each link's give-get. With a quantified chain-link, a strategy plan can move beyond hunches and guesses to achieve more by doing less, focusing on the few initiatives and activities that provide the highest return on customer value.

The fourth goal of the book is to learn from the successes and failures of the eight stories in this chapter. Some of the executive teams succeeded. Others failed, despite working with utmost dedication. By understanding the reasons for the successes and failures, readers can better synthesize and adapt best practices for themselves, their teams, and their organizations.

Finally, the book seeks to help senior executives meet the expectations CEOs have of strategy planning. Chapter 2 describes the many frustrations CEOs have with the strategy planning process and the improvements they seek. Reading this book will enable senior executives to understand their CEOs' perspectives and adapt their company's strategy planning process for greater success.

Notes

1. Barrows, Edward (2009), "Four fatal flaws of strategic planning," *Harvard Management Update*, 14(4), 1–5.
2. Grant, Robert. M. (2003), "Strategic planning in a turbulent environment: Evidence from the oil majors," *Strategic Management Journal*, 24(6), 491–517.
3. Kraus, Sascha, Rainer Harms, and Erich J. Schwarz (2006), "Strategic planning in smaller enterprises–New empirical findings," *Management Research News*, 29(6), 334–344.
4. Grant, Robert. M. (2003), "Strategic planning in a turbulent environment: Evidence from the oil majors," *Strategic Management Journal*, 24(6), 491–517.

2

The CEO Perspective on Strategy Planning

Among all the activities undertaken by CEOs none is as consequential as strategy planning.

CEOs rely on their supporting senior executives to develop and implement strategy for their companies. Senior executives typically rely on broad guidance from the chief executive but ultimately deliver strategy plans to drive company performance. A CEO then uses the strategy plan to communicate the company's mission, vision, and goals to the board. Board members use the strategy plan to hold the CEO accountable for delivering financial performance.

No matter the strategy planning approach an organization uses, CEOs and board members pay close attention to the strategy plan's ability to deliver sales growth and margins. For a CEO, strategy planning can also become a means to address a variety of issues, such as perception management and external stakeholder signaling, control, performance evaluation, pushing individual agendas and priorities, and allocating resources through budgeting.

What perspective do individual CEOs take when thinking about and evaluating the strategy planning process? What are CEOs' hopes and ambitions for their companies' strategy planning processes? How do CEOs think their companies' strategy planning processes can be improved?

V. Mittal, S. Sridhar, *Focus*, https://doi.org/10.1007/978-3-030-70720-0_2

2.1   Listening to CEOs

Multiple CEOs and private equity firm partners provided their perspectives on the strategy planning process for this book. During informal meetings, the executives answered open-ended questions about their companies' strategy planning processes. In addition to describing strategy planning, they addressed what works and what does not work in the process. Several CEOs offered access to the entire strategy planning process through meetings, breakout sessions with executive teams, and extensive debriefings to understand how and why they do what they do.

Some CEOs, engaging in strategy planning for the first time, exhibit heightened intellectual curiosity about its potential. Novice CEOs often equate strategy planning with presentations listing sales targets and qualitative assessments via established frameworks (e.g., Porter's Five Forces, or SWOT (Strengths, Weaknesses, Opportunities, and Threats), analyses). In most cases, the analyses rely on the gut feelings or hunches of mid-level or junior analysts. In almost all cases, the strategy model does not reflect deep discussions or shared understanding among senior executives.

More experienced CEOs take a nuanced view of strategy planning's potential and perils. For them, strategy planning goes beyond improving financial performance. The CEOs describe goals including: (1) using a customer, rather than internal, perspective; (2) making sense of voluminous industry, sector, and company information; (3) benchmarking position relative to competitors and marketplace; (4) focusing and sequencing senior executives' work without relying on personal preferences, biases, and positions; and (5) driving accountability and alignment among senior executives, middle management, and frontline employees.

Effective CEOs use the strategy planning process as a vehicle for change management, executive assessment, and talent development. Specifically, the process enables CEOs to observe senior executives up close and assess them in terms of critical thinking, listening ability, emotional intelligence, and conflict-management skills. From a social perspective, many CEOs value strategy retreats for enabling senior executives to learn from each other and develop a better understanding of each other's roles.

Finally, for CEOs of multidivisional companies and managing directors of private equity firms, the strategy planning process provides a comparative lens. It helps private equity partners compare and contrast the different and often disparate approaches used by their portfolio companies' CEOs. Similarly, CEOs of multidivisional companies can compare the strategy planning approaches used by their divisional, regional, and business-group presidents.

> - Internally Focused Process and No Customer Lens
> - Informed by Expensive Research That is Siloed and Bifurcated
> - Lack of Meaningful Comparisons and Benchmarking
> - A Recipe for Analysis Paralysis
> - No Way to Empirically Link Strategy to Outcomes
> - No Meaningful Way to Focus and Sequence the Work
> - Deciding the Agenda Through C-Suite's Personal Preferences, Not Customer Needs
> - Lacking a Blueprint To Drive Alignment In the Organization

Fig. 2.1 CEOs' issues with strategy planning

CEOs have plenty to say about strategy planning, and offer nuanced views about its positives and negatives. They see strategy planning as neither irredeemably flawed nor a silver bullet capable of fixing all the problems facing their companies. They see it as a complex process that can be improved to engage senior executives more meaningfully, to better leverage their ideas, and to coordinate their actions for superior results.

Across the many CEOs sharing their views for this book, eight central issues emerge as critical to successful strategy planning. And the fundamental inability of strategy planning processes to address the issues mitigates their upside. The eight issues represent eight ways in which strategy planning can be enhanced, improved, and strengthened (Fig. 2.1).

2.2 One: Lacking a Customer Lens

For many CEOs, strategy planning is internally focused. The CEO of a manufacturing and distribution company describes a process that starts with a sales target and cascades down to different departments, resulting in a series of unrelated activities. The firm's sales team decides on the appropriate prospects and initiatives to develop a sales funnel and achieve its target. The finance department develops a growth strategy of acquiring smaller companies to contribute to the sales goal. The product development group focuses on new products to contribute to sales growth. The HR group optimizes its training programs to enhance sales effectiveness.

Each group ostensibly contributes to the strategy plan by focusing on sales. The CEO, however, does not see it that way. "Despite their best efforts, each senior executive has become focused on their own group," the CEO laments.

"They all have ideas about what customers want. Some may even have talked to customers or accessed industry reports that summarize customer trends. But none of them have really brought the customers' needs squarely into the strategy planning process. They've bypassed customers and become internally focused with sales as the blanket excuse for doing so."

For another company, the strategy process starts with a two-day workshop designed to solidify its core mission, vision, and values. The company settles on integrity, safety, and innovation as its core values and "exceeding stakeholder expectations" as its mission. Each executive develops and presents a plan to infuse the values in employees' day-to-day work. "While this could motivate employees and make the executives feel good, it has ultimately become an inward-looking exercise," the CEO says. "Supposedly, a focus on the core values would motivate employees, who would then satisfy customers. The leap of logic is too large and too abstract for me to take it to my board with confidence."

2.3   Two: Informed by Siloed and Bifurcated Research That Misleads

Most companies consider strategy planning a serious exercise. In small companies with sales ranging from a few hundred thousand dollars to $20 million, CEOs often engage in strategy planning with independent consultants and a few senior executives—typically from finance and sales. They rely on internal information, such as sales trends, customer lists, qualitative strength and weakness assessments, comparative competitor analyses, mission statements, and addressing senior executives' intuitions about competencies and comparative advantages.

Larger companies typically employ a more formal strategy process involving multiple employees, consultants, and information suppliers. For example, the vice president of strategy for one oilfield services company spends several hundred thousand dollars annually on subscription information services. The services provide oil prices, global and regional supply and demand numbers, potential rig counts, and other industry trends deemed essential for forward-looking planning. The senior vice president of marketing uses research suppliers to conduct product configuration studies on current offerings and potential new launches. The executive then evaluates the company's product line and makes recommendations to the R&D group. Another supplier provides a competitor assessment using perceptual maps, value maps, and rankings of competitors on product and service attributes. The data are deemed essential to staying competitive and understanding how the firm's products fit customer needs.

The oilfield services firm's senior vice president of HR conducts an annual employee engagement study. The executive believes engaged employees are more productive and serve customers well. Internally, the vice president of sales produces monthly, quarterly, and annual forecasts for the company's CFO, providing a basis for budget planning. A team of analysts gathers information on potential projects, rates them with a "get score," and works with marketing to develop a win strategy. The team then shares a strategy report in monthly planning meetings with a careful eye on bids won and backlog.

Nearly every senior executive at the oilfield services company justifies each information report based on plausible conjectures. The HR executive justifies the million-dollar employee engagement study with assurances from consultants that engaged employees are more productive and should improve sales and profits. The marketing executive simply assumes more and better products increase sales. The oilfield company CEO, aware of the millions being spent on research, has concerns. "I cannot see how this massive amount of information improves the strategy planning process," the CEO says.

The CEO concludes much of the information fails to link the oilfield services company's strategy to desirable outcomes. The chief executive also concludes that the different studies fail to mesh together and provide a coherent narrative. The CEO believes it is critical, for example, to relate the competitor assessment study to the employee engagement study. Only then can the firm understand the relative importance of marketing and HR initiatives. As they are, the studies are siloed and bifurcated. The engagement study does not contribute to strategy planning. It only helps the HR executive make the case for increasing the employee communication and training budget. The marketing executive's competitor study might improve the customer experience, but it does not help the CEO understand how or why a customer focus can drive strategy for improved financial outcomes.

Standing back, the CEO understands his executives are advancing siloed strategy perspectives. Instead, the chief executive seeks a unified, simple, and coherent set of industry studies providing the basis for measuring strategy outcomes, incorporating customer and employee needs, and focusing on the most essential aspects of strategy.

2.4 Three: No Meaningful Comparisons

Effective CEOs understand an internal focus, bifurcation from customers and competitors, and a siloed approach preclude meaningful comparisons and benchmarks for strategy evaluation.

The CEO of one large company describes a monthly strategy meeting in 2020 in which the firm's HR executive shared the results of a flash employee survey. The survey showed 77.8% of employees were engaged, 72% felt positive about the future, and 75% believed the company handled the COVID-19 pandemic well. "Except for feel-good vibes, what does this mean?" the CEO asked at the time. "Is 70% a good rate? What is the comparable rate at key competitors—50% or 80%? More importantly, does engagement or feeling positive translate into meaningful outcomes, such as service provided to clients? What are the drivers of engagement, and how does engagement or feeling positive fit into the company's strategy?" The CEO became animated, voicing frustration at the senior executives' penchant for "throwing out bits and pieces of data without meaningful comparison or context for strategy."

Discussions with CEOs reveal several reasons for the lack of meaningful comparisons. For many companies, competitor information is simply unavailable. One company's analyses are based on information gained from competitors' websites. Each year, the company's marketing director scrapes the websites, interprets the information, and creates the strategy plan's "competitor comparison" section. "It changes from year to year simply depending on the director's subjective interpretation or the analyst who was designated with the task," the company's CEO says. "Moreover, it lacks the real information we would need for strategy planning—what is the value proposition that customers see in our offering and competitors' offering?"

Many CEOs state they need externally focused, robust benchmarking over time to track their strategy plan's performance. "The only year-over-year or quarter-over-quarter benchmarking I receive is sales," one chief executive says. "My CFO can provide me sales targets and actual sales by region and by quarter … but we have no idea about competitor sales. It would be more insightful to get customer metrics over time—quality perceptions for our offerings relative to competitors, retention rates, and so on. We spend so much on different initiatives. The operations group provides hundreds of efficiency and utilization metrics. We have too many metrics but no meaningful comparisons over time, against competitors, or across divisions." Benchmarking and tracking for a meaningful assessment of a company's standing relative to key competitors and the industry emerges as a key theme for many CEOs.

CEOs also bemoan meaningless performance indicators, benchmarks, and comparisons. Nearly all CEOs say strategy planning meetings too often turn into endless presentations about performance indicators. They say few senior executives provide an understanding of how the indicators contribute to improving performance. One company identifying safety as a core value has a group of eight analysts cross-reporting to HR and operations on safety. They compile a quarterly report on more than 30 performance indicators, such as total recordable incidents and days off. The senior vice president of HR argues the indicators improve employee engagement and contribute to margins through productivity. But the firm's CEO says no one has ever correlated safety metrics to employee engagement, productivity, and margins. When the firm finally conducts the analysis, it finds no relationship between safety metrics and employee engagement, nor between employee engagement and productivity.

2.5   Four: Analysis Paralysis

Many CEOs are dismayed not only by the voluminous information each of their functional areas produce, but also by the resources and time they take to analyze it. The firms' strategy planning processes encourage information production and utilization and lead to multiple competing interpretations. In turn, executives involved in strategy planning must sort through huge amounts of information and use their personal judgment to decide what is important, invariably injecting unproductive conflict in the process. As a result, conflict resolution becomes a central theme in many strategy planning processes.

One CEO reports asking finance to provide a cost for the firm's research studies and amount of time spent deciphering them. The chief executive is surprised to learn the company, with about $500 million in sales, is spending almost $7.3 million on gathering and interpreting information streams. Furthermore, the CEO realizes the team spends excessive time analyzing and interpreting the reports because none of them is designed to inform the strategy process. "The reports provide information that can be strategic," the senior vice president of strategy analytics says. "But that requires making a lot of inferences that may be risky, taking many leaps of faith, a lot of interpretation, and connecting-the-dots to draw conclusions for which the information is not intended in the first place. Even then, we cannot be sure that the conclusions are reliable enough to hang our strategy hat on them."

According to CEOs, excessive information leads to analysis paralysis, another frustrating strategy planning outcome. Because much of the information is not directly relevant to strategy planning, different users manipulate it for their purposes. For example, one company collects market share data by region. It ranges from 22% to 35% for the firm's six operating areas. Each regional sales team interprets the data to frame its sales efforts as successful. The region with 22% market share compares it to its prior year's 18% share, claiming success. The region with 35% highlights its large market share relative to other regions, though its prior year share is 33.2%. No group provides clear empirical evidence demonstrating that the strategic initiatives it has undertaken actually impacted sales. The company's CEO is uninterested, even though sales growth is the primary metric by which the board evaluates the executive. "[I'm] not sure if market share is a clear metric to measure sales growth, our strategic objective," the CEO says. "Market share can be had by simply lowering prices and chasing lower quality customers."

The CEO of a multidivisional, global company echoes the point. The company counts safety and sustainability as two core values, and almost every senior executive employs initiatives and performance indicators around them. The CEO says the executives discussed five indicators measuring employee absentee days for several hours during the firm's last strategy planning meeting. For the CEO, the five metrics are not appreciably different and tell essentially the same story. The CEO wonders if each metric predicts strategy outcomes relevant to shareholders or customers differently. All five indicators lead to the same conclusion.

2.6   Five: Lacking a Link Between Strategy and Financial Outcomes

Although many firms intend strategy planning to achieve performance outcomes like sales growth and margin expansion, senior executives often tell CEOs to "take their word that it [is] happening." CEOs repeatedly find executives claiming that successful outcomes result from their proposed strategies but blame unsuccessful outcomes on external events. The chief executives express frustration that, despite the massive amount of information the strategy planning process gathers, they lack a formal methodology linking strategy to outcomes.

The misalignment of strategy and performance outcomes occurs for many reasons. Some companies simply cannot agree on strategy inputs and outputs.

For example, does sales growth occur due to more motivated employees, a change in product lineup, or more aggressive sales efforts? While senior executives might suggest all three inputs affect sales growth, CEOs still lack answers to two key questions:

(1) What are the key inputs and outputs of the strategy process?
(2) How can the relative impact of each input on the desired output be calculated in a consistent, unbiased, and robust manner?

For the oilfield services company, senior executives in different functional areas simply report the firm's average ratings for a given year. "I know that 68% of my employees are engaged, my net promoter score is at 54, we introduced eight new products and won 33% of the bids submitted," the CEO says. "What I don't know—and would like to know—is how they are related to each other and how much each of these numbers contributes to strategy success. What, for example, is the relative contribution of employee engagement, promoter score, new products and bid winning to sales and margins? Do they even add to customer value or sales growth or something tangible?"

The desire to empirically link strategy inputs to strategy outcomes encapsulates the goal of making the strategy planning process measurable and repeatable over time. Effective CEOs desire a mechanism to hold senior executives accountable for the goals set during strategy planning. "We have more than 30 major strategic initiatives running in the company, each costing millions of dollars," one CEO says. "The sponsoring executive for each initiative makes a case that the initiative will improve company performance, but no one has ever measured the inputs and linked them to outputs. As the CEO, I have to take their word for it."

CEOs express disdain for simplistic models, such as those linking product improvements and price discounts to sales. They prefer realistic models that specify how operational inputs and execution levers lead to desirable outcomes, such as more satisfied customers, higher retention, and increased word-of-mouth—all of which drive sales growth. Yet, their strategy planning fails to link strategic levers to desired outcomes. "Such an empirical model should start by identifying specific variables and metrics representing strategy inputs and then statistically link the inputs to strategy outputs," one CEO says. "Then, the strategy team and senior leadership of the company would reach an agreement on how the inputs and outputs should be measured and linked. A statistical model could provide the strength of each linkage, ultimately operationalizing the strategy."

2.7   Six: No Meaningful Way to Focus and Sequence Executives' Effort

How can CEOs focus and sequence senior executives' work and attention? "I've seen strategy presentations that talk big concepts—a listing of my company's strengths and weaknesses, a qualitative assessment of stakeholder bargaining power, competitive intensity, a comparison of my company's offerings relative to competitors, and so forth," one chief executive says. "But at the end of the day, all these are constructs that are based on the judgment of an analyst and do not provide any meaningful way to focus and sequence the work of the senior leadership team. The team has to understand that strategy is really about focusing and sequencing the work—budget, initiatives, and activities—that provide the most value to customers and shareholders."

CEOs offer many methods to focus and sequence their work, and have an acute awareness of their firms' relative strengths and weaknesses—shareholder value, sales growth, employee engagement, and customer value, to name a few:

- Company boards ultimately evaluate most CEOs via shareholder value, and the chief executives understand the metric's importance. However, most CEOs acknowledge shareholder value is not easily measurable for privately owned companies and difficult to relate to strategic action for publicly owned companies, as many market factors determine stock price.
- Most CEOs believe sales is a better metric than shareholder value because it is directly measurable and more proximal to strategy planning, even if it is volatile and influenced by competitor and marketing actions. CEOs acknowledge pursuing sales growth can lead to perverse incentives. Many recount stories of sales teams chasing the wrong customers and signing unprofitable contracts to boost numbers. In many cases, well-meaning sales teams simply do not understand their company's customer-value proposition because it has not been clearly articulated. Most CEOs agree sales growth and margins should be part of their strategy plans; however, the metrics should not be the yardsticks by which they focus and sequence their work.
- Most CEOs say employee engagement is a critical input but not viable for focusing and sequencing strategic planning. CEOs acknowledge employees are critical stakeholders, especially in industries where recruitment and retention are challenging. Yet, making budgetary, initiative, and activity decisions to promote employee engagement can be misleading. Indeed, most CEOs doubt engaging employees is directly related to sales or

customer value. "If the company increases salary, lowers accountability, and does employee appreciation all the time, our employees will be more engaged," one CEO says. "Yet, how will this meaningfully contribute to strategic success?" Another CEO suggests trends like increasing employee engagement, environmental, social, and corporate governance, and diversity and inclusion are best seen as constraints needing to be managed in strategy planning, not yardsticks for focusing and sequencing the process.

- Customer value emerges as an appropriate goal for focusing and sequencing strategy planning for many CEOs. "After all, customers are the ultimate source of cash flow for my company," one CEO says. "If customers are satisfied with our offering, they will buy more, recommend more, refer more, and are less likely to defect to competitors. In the long term, providing customer value is the best insurance for sales growth and stock growth." The customer value metric enables companies to differentiate themselves from competitors and provides a framework for matching what customers want to what they will pay. It provides companies external focus and can help measure performance relative to competitors. However, some CEOs express reservations about customer value. First, they state their companies lack a consistent, credible, and repeatable way to measure customer value and determine the strategic factors driving it. Second, they lack a statistically valid and reliable way to link customer value to financial metrics like sales growth and margin. Most CEOs are aware of industry studies providing guidance on the relationships, but they are unable to extrapolate industry-level results to their specific situations. For customer value to focus and sequence strategy planning, it must therefore be linked to firm--level strategy areas and financial outcomes.

2.8   Seven: Following Executives' Personal Preferences to Define Strategy

Many CEOs acknowledge strategy planning decisions are often made based on the personal preferences, perceptions, hunches, beliefs, experiences, and biases of senior executives. Often, the approach reflects the relationship and trust the executives build with their CEOs, as well as their seniority and experience. In many cases, CEOs understand executives' solutions reflect their bias and self-interest. But in the absence of a credible way to focus and sequence strategy planning, the agenda is mired in subjectivity.

Consider the CEO of an engineering and construction company. Six months after joining the firm, the chief executive describes frustration with the director of sales planning, who has more than 20 years of tenure. The director takes information from the sales team about potential leads and creates a forecast for the vice president of finance, who uses the data to develop the next year's budget. The budget dictates the company's strategy plan. "The only problem is that the sales forecast has not been accurate for the last 17 years," the CEO says. "On average, it is off by 25–30% each quarter, and it sometimes overpredicts and sometimes underpredicts. When I brought it to the attention of the VP-Finance, he stated that there wasn't a better way in the company to make the forecast. Eventually, I had to get rid of both of them and install a new team that used predictive analytics to forecast sales. The margin of error is now more manageable at 4–6%—still not as precise, but much better."

CEOs also face difficulties when executive team members take a solitary perspective to justify their proposed solutions. "For finance, everything revolves around cost cutting," one CEO says. "HR is all about more training and employee engagement. Better branding, more marketing spending, and social media are the solution for all strategic issues, according to marketing. Manufacturing wants to impose lean sigma on all processes. My team members are all well-meaning, but the isolated perspective that is more based on their personal preferences and biases does not really bode well for … success."

The strategy planning process is often built around adjudicating the personal preferences, biases, and assumptions of individual team members. It assumes the CEO's role is to build trust and relationships so executives can question each other's assumptions without fear of reprisal. According to many CEOs, the process can be valuable during an implementation phase, when they must build confidence, commitment, and consensus among the larger employee base. "With my senior executives, the strategy process needs to focus on providing more credible, well-laid out, and thoughtful information," one CEO says. "It should be more structured and focused on using the information for making choices. It should not become a team-building exercise focused on resolving conflict and using emotional intelligence for relationship management."

The concern dovetails with another issue raised by some CEOs, as well as private equity partners. "I have some CEOs or division presidents who are not good at strategy development, [but] they implement strategies well," a private equity partner says. "Other CEOs are great at developing strategy, but they all have different ways of doing it. With no consistency, it is difficult to not only compare the quality of strategy among the different divisions or companies, but also maintain consistency over time. Just like financial reporting, it would be useful to have a data-driven strategy process that is repeatable, comparable, and transferrable across divisions, units, companies, and CEOs." In other words, CEOs need and desire a process for developing, implementing, and evaluating strategy that goes beyond individuals and stands as an independent process.

2.9   Eight: No Blueprint for Alignment

Many CEOs see strategy development and implementation as separate but interrelated. They find strategy planning strives for the "big picture" and becomes alienated from the daily grind of implementation.

"We paid a lot of money to a big consulting company to help develop strategy," one CEO says. "At the end of the day, we were left with generics: a mission and vision statement emphasizing three values—safety, sustainability, and excellence—and a few presentations by each of the SVPs on how they will strive to achieve the values. Each SVP quickly designed initiatives or repackaged existing initiatives to infuse them with the values. But no compelling or measurable implementation plan emerged. It only created more confusion, giving each SVP a license to go out and do their thing." Another CEO describes a lack of alignment among senior executives, middle managers, and frontline employees. While the company's strategy was meaningful to senior executives, it did not translate to measurable goals for middle management or specific activities for frontline employees. "What does excellence as a value mean?" the chief executive asks. "It means different things to different people at different levels in my company. At the end of the day, the strategy team needs to sort out these ambiguities and present a cohesive plan to drive alignment from top to bottom."

CEOs seek plans linking strategy areas to an overall metric predictably driving sales growth. They want to know what to prioritize and what to defer. In other words, they want specific performance metrics to measure progress in strategy areas to emphasize—not in any and every strategy area.

In one company, the strategy group finds customer value drives sales growth. In turn, customer value is driven by after-sales service. The group then develops specific initiatives in after-sales service and metrics for measuring them. The approach drives accountability throughout the company, but it also helps the CEO measure implementation effectiveness against the firm's actual strategy goal.

2.10 Conclusion

Reflecting on their experiences with strategy planning, CEOs articulate eight central challenges. The challenges are echoed by a CEO running a multi-billion-dollar, global company with several divisions, as well as the chief executive of a small outsourcing firm. As one CEO says, "strategy planning is like advertising or branding. I know that at least half of it is wasted. I just wish I knew which half."

Do the CEOs surveyed reflect a general consensus among a broad group? Even if a large number of CEOs believe strategy planning does not work, the finding does not provide conclusive evidence. Imagine a patient's view of a medical treatment. When asked, the patient may articulate all sorts of issues with the treatment, even believing it is ineffective. But what if, in reality, the patient is getting better?

Scientifically evaluating strategy planning's efficacy requires broad evidence going beyond the issues framed in a CEO survey. The next few chapters describe empirical evidence evaluating the CEOs' perspectives on the strategy planning process and its efficacy. The evidence is multifaceted and incorporates many approaches and methodologies—systematic reviews of published scientific research, observations of strategy planning and implementation in many organizations, interviews and discussions with hundreds of managers and senior executives, surveys of managers and executives conducting strategy planning, and linking survey results to financial metrics like sales, margins, efficiency, and return on investment.

Imagine again the medical patient. Rather than relying on the patient's view of a medical treatment, evidence must be used to correlate its effects on health. For CEOs, evidence can likewise correlate the strategy planning process to financial outcomes. The evidence evaluates the extent to which strategy planning helps senior executives realize critical goals, such as weaving the customer perspective into strategy, aligning senior executives with middle managers and frontline employees, evaluating the contribution of strategy planning to financial performance, determining which initiatives to enact and which to defer, and focusing and sequencing senior executives' work.

3

The Perils and Promise of Strategy Planning

Strategy planning is costly. Some large companies have multiple strategy plans at the corporate, divisional, and even regional levels. Preparing a strategy plan involves time and effort from executives and managers in each company unit, as well as additional effort gathering data, information, and plan inputs. It involves dedicated in-house resources (e.g., chief strategy officers and staff) or costly outside consultants. In a study of oil and gas company strategy planning, researchers found ExxonMobil used 370 strategy planning staff members for 13 business groups as far back as 1995.[1] In 2003, the 416-person strategy planning staff at Italian oil and gas company Eni vastly outnumbered the regular corporate staff of 72 employees.

The direct and indirect costs of strategy planning have been reported to run anywhere from hundreds of thousands to many millions of dollars, according to management consultant Peter McCann. Speaking on a Web-based message board in 2016, McCann estimated the cost at about one-quarter of 1% of sales. Accordingly, for an established, highly complex, multidivisional, multinational organization like a major bank, out-of-pocket strategy planning costs may be in excess of $10 million. Internal costs may double the number.

3.1 What CEOs Believe

In private, many seasoned executives are wary of strategy planning processes. During a strategy forum, the president of a multi-million-dollar division stated, "Whenever I hear the word 'strategic,' I grab my wallet." Lou Gerstner,

© The Author(s), under exclusive license to Springer Nature Switzerland AG 2021
V. Mittal, S. Sridhar, *Focus*, https://doi.org/10.1007/978-3-030-70720-0_3

former IBM CEO, asked fellow chief executives about strategy planning in 1972 and received the following reactions:[2]

- "Strategic planning is basically just a plaything of staff."
- "Strategic planning? A staggering waste of time and money."

Gerstner concluded: "Some CEOs would disagree with these comments, and certainly few, if any, would agree publicly. But the fact remains that in the large majority of companies, corporate planning tends to be an academic, ill-defined activity with little or no bottom-line impact."[3]

In a 2003 *Sloan Management Review* article, Sarah Kaplan and Eric Beinhocker reported a similar sentiment from executives regarding formal strategy planning:[4]

- "Our planning process is like a primitive … ritual. No one is exactly sure why we do it, but there is an almost mystical hope that something good will come out of it."
- "It's like the old communist system: We pretend to make strategy, and they pretend to follow it."

In a 2006 *Harvard Business Review* article, executives lobbed other complaints about the value of a yearly strategy planning process. They ranged from "It takes too much time" to "It's disconnected from the way we run the business."[5]

3.2   What Senior Executives and Managers Believe

Several surveys document senior executives' and managers' beliefs about strategy planning. The qualitative complaints about strategy planning are consistent with the results of a 2006 *McKinsey Quarterly* survey conducted among 796 managers worldwide.[6] The survey showed a surprising level of disillusionment, dissatisfaction, and disagreement among respondents about the strategy planning process. First, managers were often not privy to their companies' strategy planning:

- Only 34% of respondents believed important strategy decisions were made in a formal planning process. And 52% of respondents believed a small senior group, including the CEO, made all important strategy decisions.
- Knowledge about the strategy planning process helped managers feel better about where their company was headed. Among the 34% of respondents who believed important strategy decisions were made via a formal planning process, 79% said it played a somewhat significant, very significant, or extremely significant role in framing their company's strategy plan.

Second, some survey respondents believed strategy planning did not work well for their specific company. Only

- 64% of respondents believed strategy planning led to decisions allowing their company to meet goals and challenges;
- 57% believed the strategy planning process was fact-based;
- 53% believed strategy planning focused on strategy, not tactical issues;
- 35% felt they received worthwhile analyses and information at the right time in the process; and
- 20% believed the process was efficient.

Third, a lack of confidence in strategy planning brought out a wide range of suggestions from managers to improve the process:

- *Focus*—31% of participants said the first thing they would do to improve strategy planning would be to find a way to identify and focus on the most important issues.
- *Alignment*—37% of participants said the first thing they would do would be to align strategy planning and execution.
- *Accountability*—32% of participants said the first thing they would do would be to monitor whether their company actually achieved its strategic plan.

Fourth, the issues of focus, alignment, and accountability resonated as utopian goals, given the state of decision-making in organizations. For example,

- 55% of participants believed discussion about how to implement strategy planning resulted in progress toward an effective strategy;
- 49% indicated they felt free to discuss difficult issues openly and honestly;
- 20% indicated they were willing to put aside their personal agendas; and

- 56% said their company tracked strategic initiative execution; therefore, strategy initiatives were not believed to be tracked in 44% of cases.

The 2006 *McKinsey Quarterly* survey also corroborated findings from a strategy assessment conducted at several companies, including FACILITYCO and ABCO. (See Chap. 1 for more information about the firms.) The FACILITYCO executive team was comprised of 65 individuals; 12 executives made up the team at ABCO. Each executive, including the CEOs, anonymously wrote what they believed were their company's top three strategy objectives. The percentage of executives who agreed on the top-three strategy objectives articulated by the CEO (Fig. 3.1) were as follows:

- 10% agreed with zero objectives.
- 54% agreed with one objective.
- 36% agreed with two objectives.
- 0% agreed with all three objectives.

The pattern of results is not unique to FACILITYCO and ABCO, and disagreement among executives manifests in many dysfunctional outcomes. At the most basic level, the executive team becomes mired in politics, firefighting, and daily tasks, rather than focusing on improving and implementing strategy.

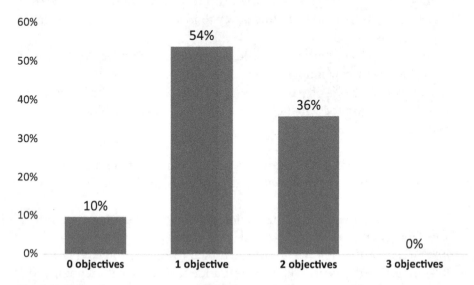

Fig. 3.1 Executives' agreement with CEOs' top-three strategy objectives

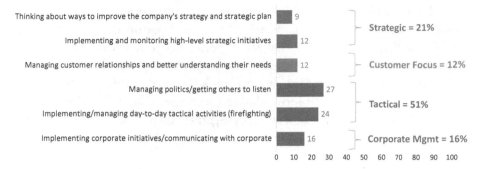

Fig. 3.2 Time executives spend on activities/areas

FACILITYCO and ABCO executives also reported the time they spent on different activities. The results, shown in Fig. 3.2, surprised the companies' CEOs, who expected their executives to spend at least two-thirds of their time on strategy. Instead, executives spent half their time (51%) on tactical activities, politics, and firefighting. They spent only 21% of their time thinking about ways to improve their company's strategy plan or implementing it. Customer relationships and corporate relationships consumed the remainder of their time.

The results capture the paradox of strategy planning. CEOs, senior executives, and managers often state publicly that strategy planning is important and they fully believe in and support their company's strategy plan. Privately, however, their beliefs and actions do not follow the pronouncements. Not only do they disagree with their CEOs' most important strategy objectives, but they spend time on tasks unrelated to strategy. And their beliefs and behaviors lead to strategy having low impact on company performance. The FACILITYCO and ABCO survey results are also consistent with the nuanced—and often negative—CEO perspective of strategy planning presented in Chap. 2.

3.3 Executives' Subjective Beliefs and Objective Reality

To evaluate the promise of strategy planning, imagine two groups of companies. One group engages in strategy planning. The other does not. If strategy planning delivers, it should at least show a positive correlation with financial returns. That is, the group of companies conducting strategy planning should perform better financially than the control group.

To better understand the issue, one can first examine executives' beliefs about financial performance and their firm's actual performance—subjective versus objective performance. Subjective performance refers to a company's performance as perceived by executives. To measure it, executives provide their subjective assessment of their company's financial metrics, such as ROI, sales, margins, and profitability, relative to competitors. Objective performance relies on secondary data; an analyst gathers data on a firm's actual sales from financial records, accounting-based profits, cash flow, stock price, and other metrics.

Observing the associations between subjective beliefs about a company's performance and objective performance can provide an assessment of the firm's strategy planning:

- If companies implementing strategy planning show better subjective and objective performance than companies with no formal planning process, one can conclude strategy planning works and executives believe in it. The condition is like a functioning medicine in a clinical trial. The pill works, and patients believe it works.
- If companies implementing strategy planning do not show better objective performance than companies with no strategy planning, but their executives believe performance is improved, one can conclude a placebo effect. The executives believe the medicine works, but it is in fact a sugar pill.
- Strategy planning might have no association with subjective performance but a positive association with objective performance. This is analogous to a fully functioning medicine that patients do not believe in.
- If strategy planning has no association with either subjective or objective performance, it is like a nonfunctioning placebo medication that fails to fool patients.

Prior to a formal evaluation of strategy planning among test subjects, one would expect a strong positive association with both subjective and objective financial performance. That is, strategy planning should not only improve actual financial performance, but executives should also believe in its effectiveness.

Extensive academic studies over 70 years have examined strategy planning's effectiveness. The studies, mostly published in peer-reviewed journals, have used many methodologies, looked at companies in different sectors and countries, and spanned different time periods. Yet, they have arrived at roughly the same conclusion. Overall, they show a weak or nonexistent link between strategy planning and firm performance.[7]

One early study investigating strategy planning in the manufacturing sector is indicative. Including chemical, oil and gas, food, machinery, and steel companies, the study proposed a strong association between strategy planning and financial performance, but it lacked internal validity. The purported association could have been attributed to a variety of factors, such as managerial talent and industry changes, rather than strategy planning.[8]

Combing through other studies shows the same pattern of results. A study of small U.S. banks found those without formal strategy planning systems performed just as well as those with formal plans.[9] Having a formal strategy planning system did not improve performance. The researchers highlighted other studies, among 21 large U.K. firms[10] and Fortune 500 companies[11] and a survey of Fortune 1000 CEOs,[12] showing either no association or a negative association between strategy planning and financial performance. Taken together, the studies found no statistically reliable evidence for strategy planning enhancing firms' finances.

A systematic review of studies published over the last 70 years conducted for this book examined the link between strategy planning and firm performance. The review uncovered 58 studies that looked at 758 associations between the planning process and financial results. The correlations were based on data from a total of 58,456 managers, and the results were based on a large database of firms and managers representing many different:

- industries, including automotive, banking, chemicals, durable goods, food, machinery, manufacturing, oil and gas, pharmaceuticals, service sector, and steel;
- regions, including Asia (India, Japan, Turkey, and Sri Lanka), Africa (Morocco), Australia, Europe (the United Kingdom, France, and the Netherlands), North America (the United States and Canada), and South America (Brazil);
- participants, including top executives and senior managers, and statistical links between formal strategy planning and objective financial performance;
- performance metrics, like growth and productivity, performance relative to competitors, market share, top-line metrics (sales and sales growth), bottom-line measures (profits, return on assets, and profit growth), and stock market metrics (stock price and book value per share); and
- publications, including research journals and practitioner outlets from many fields, such as strategy, entrepreneurship, marketing, organizational behavior, finance, operations, small business research, and accounting.

Of the 758 correlations, only 717 could be retained for analysis due to study characteristics. Each correlation was classified based on two factors:

- *Objective versus subjective performance measures*: A correlation was deemed based on objective performance if it used performance data gathered from secondary sources like income statements, stock market metrics, actual sales records, ROI/ROA, margins, and profits from financial statements. Other correlations were based on subjective data from executives' perceptions of performance. (To gather such subjective assessments of performance, executives fill out surveys indicating how they believe their company is performing in absolute terms and relative to competitors.)
- *Financial versus nonfinancial performance metrics*: Financial performance metrics include outcomes such as sales, margins, EBITDA, stock price, and ROA/ROI, among others. In contrast, nonfinancial metrics may include outcomes such as employee engagement, market growth, sustainability, recognition by other executives, and rankings (e.g., *Forbes*).

One way to understand the data is to think of a pharmaceutical company conducting clinical trials to test the efficacy of a drug. Suppose the pharmaceutical company conducts 58 clinical trials and uncovers 717 correlations between administering a medicine and patient outcomes. Administering or not administering the medicine is akin to conducting strategy planning versus not doing so. In the analogy, patient outcomes are similar to firm performance. Patient outcomes can be measured in terms of medical or nonmedical consequences (financial or nonfinancial outcomes) and in terms of subjective or objective metrics.

To understand whether a medicine is effective, one can ask a variety of questions, such as: Of the 717 times the effect of the medicine on patient outcomes is measured, how many times does it make the patient worse (negative effect) or better (positive effect)? How many times does it have no effect on the patient's health (zero effect)? In the same way, one can ask about strategy planning's effectiveness. Of the 717 studies examined for the present analysis, 75% of the correlations ($n = 534$) were statistically the same as zero, showing no association between strategy planning and performance, and 4% ($n = 29$) were statistically negative, that is, less than zero. In other words, in 79% of cases, strategy planning had no association or a negative association with performance. In only 21% of the cases ($n = 154$) was strategy planning positively and significantly associated with performance. This is similar to a pharmaceutical company finding 717 correlations in clinical trials testing the efficacy of a drug and 75% showing the medication does not improve patient

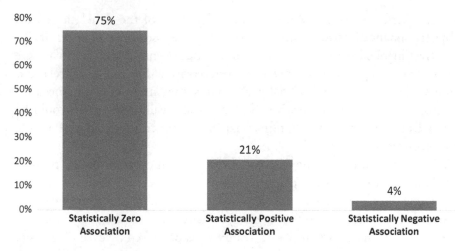

Fig. 3.3 Association between strategy planning and performance outcomes

Table 3.1 Strategy planning effectiveness by measure type

	Financial		Nonfinancial	
	Subjective	Objective	Subjective	Objective
Zero association	196 (74%)	313 (82%)	24 (36%)	1 (50%)
Negative association	11 (4%)	16 (4%)	2 (3%)	0
Positive association	57 (22%)	55 (14%)	41 (61%)	1 (50%)
Total	264 (100%)	384 (100%)	67 (100%)	2 (100%)

health, 4% showing the drug diminishes patient health, and 21% showing the drug improves patient health. Under the circumstances, it would be difficult to imagine doctors prescribing the medication or patients wanting to take it. With similar evidence for the effectiveness of traditional strategy planning, why would companies want to undertake it? (Fig. 3.3)

A second way to answer the question of strategy planning's effectiveness is based on outcome type: subjective versus objective and financial versus nonfinancial. For this purpose, the 717 correlations were broken down into four groups based on whether they used subjective/objective performance measures or financial/nonfinancial performance measures. Within each category, the percentage of correlations that were positive, negative, or zero was tabulated. The results are shown in Table 3.1.

The subjective measures shown in Table 3.1 were obtained primarily from surveys or interviews with executives, in which they provided their opinion of performance. In contrast, objective measures were based on external data, such as income statements and stock market performance. Table 3.1 shows that strategy planning had a zero or negative association with subjective financial performance in 78% of cases. Only 22% of the correlations with subjective financial performance showed a positive association. The results for objective financial performance were similar but even more stark: 86% were either zero or negative, and only 14% were positive. For the 67 correlations using subjective and nonfinancial performance measures, 39% were negative or zero, while 61% were positive. No statistically valid conclusion could be drawn from the objective, nonfinancial performance measures due to the small correlation sample.

What conclusion does the data support? The chances of finding a positive association between strategy planning and financial performance—subjective or objective—is low (14% or 22%) compared to the chances of finding a zero or negative correlation (74% or 82%). Firms using strategy planning to improve financial performance—in reality or as perceived by executives—are more likely to be disappointed. Using the medical trials analogy, strategy planning turns out to be a medication likely to disappoint the patient in three out of four cases, as it will either make outcomes worse or leave them unchanged.

A third way to answer the question would be to ask: "What is the correlation between strategy planning and performance outcomes?" The correlation between two numbers can range from -1 to +1 and include 0. According to established guidelines for interpreting correlations,[13] correlations above 0 but less than 0.20 are positive and weak, those between 0.20 and 0.30 are positive and medium, and those above 0.30 are positive and strong. Similarly, correlations between 0 and -0.20 are negative and weak, those between -0.21 and -0.30 are negative and medium, and those less than -0.30 are negative and strong. It is instructive to consider the overall correlation between strategy planning and performance and break it down into the four subgroups dictated by metric type.

After adjusting for sample size, the correlation between strategy planning and performance was 0.12, with a 95% confidence interval of 0.11 to 0.13. On average, the correlation between strategy planning and performance was weak, albeit positive, at 0.12. The correlations for the four subgroups are shown in Table 3.2.

The present study examined 384 correlations (54% of the total number) between strategy planning and objective financial performance metrics. Adjusting for sample size, the average correlation was 0.11, with a 95% confidence interval of 0.09 to 0.12. Therefore, one can be 95% confident the correlation in the population represented lies between 0.09 and 0.12. The overall correlation was therefore weak, meaning strategy planning is a dismal tool for

Table 3.2 Strategy planning effectiveness incidence by measure type

	Financial measure	Nonfinancial measure
Objective measure	Number of studies = 384 Adjusted correlation = 0.11 Confidence interval = [0.09, 0.12]	Number of studies = 2 Adjusted correlation = NA Confidence Interval = NA
Subjective measure	Number of studies = 264 Adjusted correlation = 0.10 Confidence interval = [0.09, 0.12]	Number of studies = 67 Adjusted correlation = 0.19 Confidence interval = [0.17, 0.22]

improving objective financial performance. The 264 correlations between strategy planning and subjective financial performance were also weak. The average correlation was 0.10, with a 95% confidence interval of 0.09 to 0.12.

Sixty-seven of the correlations were based on subjective and nonfinancial performance measures. At 0.19, with a 95% confidence interval of 0.17 to 0.22, the average correlation was stronger than the previous measures. However, it was still weak based on accepted standards.

What is the main takeaway? Going back to the medical analogy, strategy planning is akin to a medicine that can be assessed in terms of clinical outcomes or nonclinical outcomes. Similarly, the effectiveness of strategy planning can be assessed based on financial or nonfinancial outcomes. Strategy planning has a negative or no effect in 75% of cases and is weakly correlated at 0.10 to 0.11 with financial outcomes. Even in the case of nonfinancial outcomes using subjective measures, the correlation is weak at 0.19.

3.4 Three Studies of Executive Beliefs

To better understand the association between strategy planning and firm performance, a series of surveys measured executive beliefs.

Study 1: Survey of executive MBA students. The survey asked 57 senior executives enrolled in a U.S. executive MBA program how strong an association they expected between strategy planning and sales. The respondents generally had senior roles at their companies: 64% had 15 or more years of experience, 95% had a masters or doctoral degree, and 34% were vice presidents or at a higher position (see Fig. 3.4).

The survey responses ranged from 1 to 7, where 1 was strongly disagree and 7 was strongly agree. As shown in Fig. 3.5, the results indicated confusion and skepticism about strategy planning:

Function	Percent	Number of Employees	Percent	Title	Percent
Oil and gas	48%	2,001+	58%	CEO/President	9%
Construction	11%	501-2,000	14%	Senior Vice President / Vice President	21%
Engineering	5%	50-500	16%	COO	4%
Chemical	5%	Fewer than 50	12%	Director	26%
Healthcare	5%			Manager / Analyst	38%
Other	26%			No answer	2%
Work Experience	**Percent**	**Revenue**		**Level of Education**	**Percent**
Fewer than 10 years	2%	Less than 10 million	16%	Masters/PhD	94%
10-15 years	35%	11-50 million	8%	MD/JD/other degree	2%
15-20 years	34%	51-200 million	7%	Undergraduate	4%
20-25 years	18%	200 million-2 billion	18%		
More than 25 years	11%	Over 2 billion	51%		

Fig. 3.4 Executive MBA student survey's respondent profile

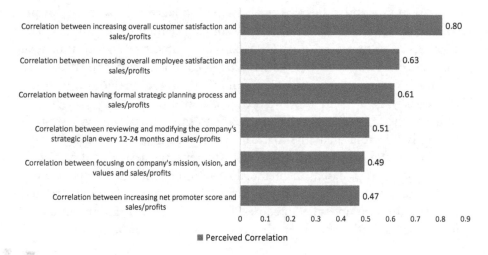

Fig. 3.5 Executives' opinions on strategy planning

- 79% agreed (6) or strongly agreed (7) their company had a formal strategy plan.
- 72% agreed or strongly agreed they were very familiar with their company's strategy plan, and 71% agreed or strongly agreed they fully understood their company's strategy objectives.
- 70% agreed or strongly agreed their company's strategy plan aligned with customer needs, and 44% agreed or strongly agreed their company's strategy plans aligned with employee needs.
- 25% agreed or strongly agreed they were "quite skeptical" of their company's plans, and 17% agreed or strongly agreed their strategy plan was "just a yearly budget update."

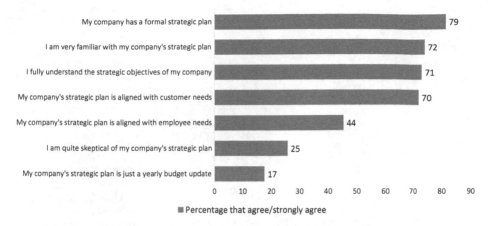

Fig. 3.6 Executives' perception of correlation between strategy goals and sales/profits

The response was more emphatic when respondents were asked to guess the correlation between their company's strategy plan and financial performance (see Fig. 3.6). On average, respondents believed the correlation between

- focusing on the company's mission, vision, and values and increasing sales and profits was 0.49;
- reviewing and modifying the company's strategic plan every one-to-two years and increasing sales and profits was 0.51; and
- having a formal strategy and increasing sales and profits was 0.6.

The results are at odds with published academic research. Recall the literature analysis conducted for this book found a positive correlation in only 21% of the studies linking strategy planning to financial performance. The average correlation between strategy planning and subjective or objective financial performance was 0.12. The MBA students in the sample therefore overestimated the association between strategy planning and financial performance by a factor of at least five. In some cases, they overestimated by a factor of eight.

Study 2: Survey of executives participating in a strategy forum. A survey of 56 senior executives attending a strategy forum in Houston in May 2018 corroborates the MBA student results. Among the executives, 15% were from oil and gas manufacturing companies, 42% were from engineering and construction companies serving oil and gas firms, and 43% were from other sectors. The executives rated the impact of strategy planning on increasing company sales and margins on a three-point scale—high, medium, and low. Figure 3.7 shows the results. Only 48% of executives felt their company's strategy plan

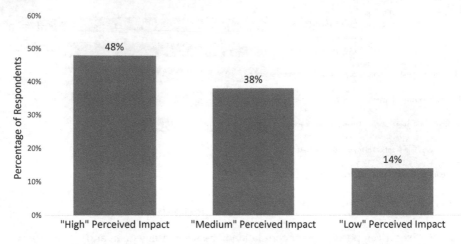

Fig. 3.7 Executives' perceived impact of strategy planning

had high impact on growing sales/margins, while 14% felt their company's strategy plan had low impact on growing sales/margins. By sector, 63% of oil and gas manufacturing executives, 54% of engineering and construction executives, and 33% of executives from other industries felt their company's strategy plan had high impact on growing sales/margins.

Study 3: Survey of directors/vice presidents participating in an energy industry advisory group. Twenty-three senior executives attended an energy strategy forum in Houston in August 2018. They filled out the same survey given to the executive MBA students in Study 1. As shown in Fig. 3.8, respondents in the group believed the correlation between

- developing a strategy plan and increasing sales and profits was as high as 0.74;
- having a formal strategy and increasing sales and profits was 0.59;
- focusing on the company's mission, vision, and values and increasing sales and profits was 0.51; and
- reviewing and modifying the company's strategy plan every 12 to 24 months and increasing sales and profits was 0.46.

In all three studies, executives overestimated the association between strategy planning and financial outcomes. Figure 3.9 shows Study 3 participants' agreement with various statements:

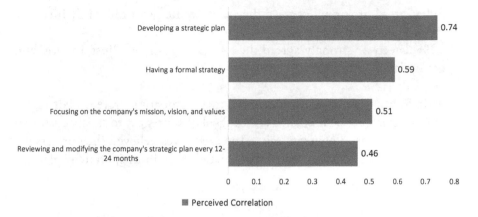

Fig. 3.8 Advisory group's beliefs about strategy planning and sales/profits

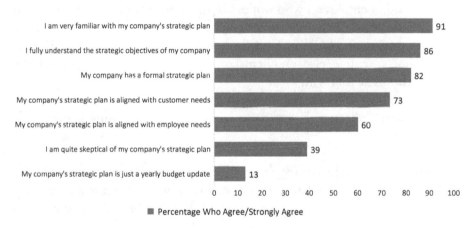

Fig. 3.9 Survey of energy industry advisory group

- 82% of respondents agreed or strongly agreed their company had a formal strategy plan.
- 91% agreed or strongly agreed they were very familiar with their company's strategy plan, and 86% agreed or strongly agreed they fully understood their company's needs.
- 60% agreed or strongly agreed their company's strategy plan aligned with employee needs, and 73% strongly agreed their company's strategy plan aligned with customer needs.

- 39% agreed or strongly agreed they were "quite skeptical" of their company's strategy plan.
- 13% agreed or strongly agreed their strategy plan was "just a yearly budget update."

As in Study 1, the executives believed their company's strategy plan aligned with customer needs. After all, a critical goal of strategy is to satisfy customers and maximize cash flow from sales. The executives believed they understood their customers' needs and fully incorporated them in their strategy planning process.

3.5   National Study of Executive Beliefs

A total of 5,433 employees who worked in full-time positions participated in a national strategy benchmark survey conducted during the fourth quarter of 2020. Among them, 668 participants were senior executives—CEO/president, senior/executive vice president, or vice president. Highlights of the results include the following:

- Participants indicated the extent to which strategy planning is correlated with sales:

  - Among the 5,433 participants, 55% stated strategy planning and sales were positively correlated; 44% stated they were not correlated or they did not know if they were correlated. Only 1% believed they were negatively correlated.
  - Among the 668 executives, 59% stated strategy planning and sales were positively correlated; 39% stated they were not correlated or they did not know if they were correlated. Only 2% believed they were negatively correlated.
  - About two of five employees and senior executives were doubtful strategy planning was consequential for sales growth.

- Participants indicated the correlation between strategy planning and sales. Only 1% of the employees and executives indicated the correct correlation of 0.12, as determined in the academic literature study. Specifically, 51 of 5433 employees and seven of 668 executives indicated the correct correlation.

- The national sample of 668 executives indicated their agreement with a series of statements about strategy planning:

  - 43% somewhat agreed or completely agreed they were doubtful about the effectiveness of their company's strategy plan.
  - 82% somewhat agreed or completely agreed senior executives in their company fully understood its strategy objectives.
  - 76% somewhat agreed or completely agreed senior executives in their company agreed about key strategy priorities.
  - 68% somewhat agreed or completely agreed frontline employees in their company fully understood its strategy objectives.
  - 67% somewhat agreed or completely agreed their company's strategy plan demonstrated where the firm stood relative to key competitors.
  - 44% somewhat agreed or completely agreed their strategy plan was just a yearly budget update.

- The national sample of 668 executives indicated the percentage of time they spent on different activities in a typical week:

  - 24% of their time was spent on strategy activities, including thinking about ways to improve their company's strategy and strategy plan, as well as implementing and monitoring high-level strategy initiatives.
  - 44% of their time was spent on non-strategy activities, including day-to-day tactical efforts, unproductive tasks/meetings, politics/firefighting, and convincing others to listen to their point of view.
  - Executives spent nearly twice as much time on non-strategy activities than strategy activities—44% versus 24%.

3.6 FACILITYCO Executives' Beliefs and Customer Needs

FACILITYCO's strategy plan emphasized safety as a core value and sales/bidding as the key driver of cash flow. Senior executives repeatedly stated they had spent significant time with corporate clients who said they valued safety highly. Hence, FACILITYCO believed its strategy emphasis on safety supported its clients' corporate values. The emphasis on sales and bidding emanated from a need to meet the revenue goals set by the CFO. The financial officer set FACILITYCO's annual sales target to meet a specified growth rate, and the sales team increased spending on sales/bidding to win new business and meet revenues.

Yet FACILITYCO, which served customers at more than 5,000 facilities worldwide, had never undertaken a systematic client study. To test whether the firm's strategy was indeed aligned with client needs, the company launched two studies:

1. In a strategy assessment, FACILITYCO's senior executives ranked eight specific client needs presumably driving customer value and sales. The executives rated their agreement with the statement, "Our strategy plan is aligned with client needs." Sixty-one percent agreed.
2. In a client assessment, FACILITYCO's customers weighted the importance of the same eight needs ranked by the executives.

If FACILITYCO's strategy plan was aligned with and supportive of client needs, the executives' rankings should have been highly correlated with customers' rankings. Table 3.3 shows the rankings by executives and clients. The correlation between the two columns is statistically no different than zero. Executives' beliefs about the rank of client needs were unrelated to clients' weights of their own needs.

FACILITYCO's executives were stunned. The premise of their strategy plan was to grow sales by meeting their two most critical customer needs—an effective sales and bidding process, and safety. Yet they were ignoring their clients and focusing on two areas salient to them. FACILITYCO's executives, despite their best intentions, had become inwardly focused.

Table 3.3 Misalignment of FACILITYCO executives and customers

	Importance ranking by	
	Senior executives	Customers
Ongoing service and support	6	1
Product/service quality	3	2
Pricing and billing	4	3
Safety	1	4
Initial sales/bidding	1	5
Client communication	5	8
Project management	7	8
Sustainability and social responsibility	8	8

The results replicate across many companies, despite senior executives' strong belief that their strategy is fully aligned with their customers' most pressing needs.

3.7   Mitigating Perils and Maximizing Promise

Strategy planning has a lower association with objective performance than with executives' performance perceptions. Managers and executives overestimate the association between strategy planning and financial metrics by a factor of at least three and as great as six. When it comes to improving financial performance, strategy planning is akin to a sugar pill or placebo. Patients believe the treatment is helping them when it is not. Even as executives maintain a strong belief that strategy planning improves their firm's financial performance, they are unsure of how or why it does so. The paradox echoes the CEO concerns outlined in Chap. 2. The CEOs believe strategy planning can only achieve its potential if the executives involved can address issues disrupting the process.

Executives and managers severely misjudge the extent to which they correctly incorporate customer needs in their company's strategy plan. In most cases, executives' perceptions of customer needs do not align with the importance placed on needs by customers. In most studies, results show a zero or negative correlation between executives' perceptions of customers' needs and their actual needs.

In an executive education course, senior executives from an engineering, procurement, and construction company—its CEO, senior vice president of sales, chief commercial officer, CFO, and CMO—described listening to the CEO of one of their main clients. At the conclusion of a one-and-a-half-hour discussion, the client's CEO was frustrated that he was unable to reach the executive team. "I don't know how much clearer I can be," he said. "All I want is a Honda or Toyota that does the job and is no-frills. And you guys keep trying to sell me a fully loaded Ferrari with all the bells and whistles I don't want and cannot pay for." Paradoxically, the meeting's purpose was to listen to the client and generate insights to drive the firm's strategy. The company has since gone bankrupt.

How can executives resolve their planning paradoxes to realize the promise of strategy planning and mitigate its perils? First, they must understand the strategy planning process their organization uses. Chapters 4, 5, and 6 describe the three dominant modalities of strategy planning most companies use: mission-vision based planning, budget-based planning, and adhocratic planning. Every organization uses one or some combination of the three modes. Each planning process brings its own assumptions, constraints, and inhibitors, which impede well-meaning executives' realization of the strategy plan's promise.

Second, senior executives must understand how to overcome the perils of each strategy planning process. The perils stem from a variety of inhibitors, outlined in Chap. 7. Some inhibitors spring from personal biases, but many result from strategy processes failing to incorporate systematic analyses of statistical relationships. Overcoming the inhibitors requires a company to use a strategy planning process relying on science to correctly represent the strategy as a series of inputs driving desirable outputs. The process eschews endless guessing and imbues strategy planning with specific facilitators. Chapter 8 describes the facilitators, which companies can use to overcome their strategy planning inhibitors, address the issues raised by CEOs in Chap. 2, and achieve the promise of strategy planning.

Third, executives can learn from others' failures and successes. Among the eight companies described in Chap. 1, some have continued to drift sideways, some have gravitated toward failure, and some have become successful. What has caused the changes? What roles have the CEOs and executives played in setting a path toward success or failure? Chapter 9 describes the successes and failures among the eight companies, and Chap. 10 provides concluding remarks.

Notes

1. Grant, Robert. M. (2003), "Strategic planning in a turbulent environment: Evidence from the oil majors," *Strategic Management Journal*, 24(6), 491–517.
2. Gerstner, Louis (1973), "Can strategic planning pay off?" *McKinsey Quarterly*, December 1.
3. Gerstner, Louis (1973), "Can strategic planning pay off?" McKinsey Quarterly, December 1.
4. Kaplan, Sarah, and Eric D. Beinhocker (2003), "The real value of strategic planning," *MIT Sloan Management Review*, 44(2), 71–76.
5. Mankins, Michael, and Richard Steele (2006), "Stop making plans; Start making decisions," *Harvard Business Review*, January, 84(1), 76–84.
6. Dye, Renee, and Olivier Sibony (2007), "How to improve strategic planning," *McKinsey Quarterly*, 3, August 1, 40–48.

7. Mintzberg, Henry (1994), "The fall and rise of strategic planning," *Harvard Business Review* 72(1), January-February, 107–114.

Pearce, John A., Elizabeth B. Freeman, and Richard B. Robinson, Jr. (1987), "The tenuous link between formal strategic planning and financial performance," *Academy of Management Review* 12(4), 658–675.

Robinson Jr., Richard B., and John A. Pearce (1983), "The impact of formalized strategic planning on financial performance in small organizations," *Strategic Management Journal*, 4(3), 197–207.

8. Thune, Stanley, and Robert House (1970), "Where long-range planning pays off—Findings of a survey of formal and informal planners," *Business Horizons*, 13(4), 81–87.

9. Robinson Jr., Richard B., and John A. Pearce (1983), "The impact of formalized strategic planning on financial performance in small organizations," *Strategic Management Journal*, 4(3), 197–207.

10. Grinyer, P. H., and David Norburn (1975), "Planning for existing markets: perceptions of chief executives and financial performance," *The Journal of the Royal Statistical Society*, January, 138(1), Series A (General), 70–97.

11. Kudla, Ronald J. (1980), "The effects of strategic planning on common stock returns," *Academy of Management Journal*, 23(1), 5–20.

12. Leontiades, Milton, and Ahmet Tezel (1980), "Planning perceptions and planning results," *Strategic Management Journal*, 1(1), 65–75.

13. Hemphill, James F. (2003), "Interpreting the magnitudes of correlation coefficients," *American Psychologist*, 58(1), January, 78–79.

4

The Inspirational Executive: Strategy Planning Through Mission, Vision, and Values

Corporate functions like financial accounting and reporting are highly regulated and follow a similar and structured approach across all types of companies. In contrast, strategy planning processes vary dramatically in style and formality. Some companies use an annual strategy retreat, while others rely on quarterly budgets to create and enforce strategy plans. Still other companies use a mix of both. Strategy planning at some companies is a highly formal process resulting in a formal document. In companies using an adaptive or entrepreneurial perspective, the strategy plan resides in a series of ongoing goals and targets for senior executives.

While strategy plans and planning processes differ widely, most firms use one of three general styles.[1] The styles include culture-based planning, budget-based planning, and adhocracy-based planning. Most companies use a combination of the approaches, with one dominating the rest. In the end, all three approaches to strategy planning are predicated on using available inputs (e.g., time, talent, money, and processes) to achieve a set of desirable outcomes (e.g., customer value, revenue, sales growth, and shareholder value).

A culture-based approach to strategy planning relies on an organization's mission, vision, and values to inspire and align stakeholders to grow sales and revenues. A budget-based approach sets budgetary targets that become the basis of executives' plans to cut costs or implement initiatives to increase revenues. An adhocracy-based approach, typically used in small companies and startups, relies on the CEO's ability to drive activities to fulfil the organization's salient goals, which can range from product commercialization to sales growth.

© The Author(s), under exclusive license to Springer Nature Switzerland AG 2021
V. Mittal, S. Sridhar, *Focus*, https://doi.org/10.1007/978-3-030-70720-0_4

Each approach draws on different executive personas. Think of an executive with a charismatic and inspirational personality who can motivate a team with a mission that inspires them. The culture-based approach personifies the inspirational executive, who can identify an underlying vision and values to inspire a company's employees to execute strategy. In contrast, an analytical executive can rally the team by providing detailed financial projections, budgets, and accountability. Thus, a budget-based approach to strategy personifies the analytical executive, who uses such financial goals to help the team develop and evaluate strategy projects and initiatives. In other words, the team ensures success by meeting its budget goals. Finally, a do-it-all executive provides the necessary impetus to team members by inspiring them, providing them short- and long-term goals, and helping execute. The adhocratic approach, then, emanates from a kind of "superhuman" executive who can take on everything—goal setting, planning, and executing.

For any senior executive developing or implementing strategy, it is important to understand the approach used. Each strategy planning approach brings its own promise and perils as it seeks to focus an organization's resources to achieve specific outcomes.

4.1   Understanding the Inspirational Approach

The inspirational approach to strategy planning is founded on senior executives articulating the mission, vision, and values of their organization. The concept of generating a corporate mission, vision, and values statement goes back to the 1920s, coinciding with the origin of branding and modern corporations. Rooted in anthropology, corporate values and mission statements explain a company's professional ethos and ingrained culture to internal and external stakeholders.

Just like a brand, the mission, vision, and values of a company seek to embody its underlying ethos—what it stands for—for various constituents. Some firms use "corporate branding" interchangeably with their core mission, vision, and values.[2] Often, a company's corporate brand or culture, as reflected in its mission, vision, and values, defines the "pattern of assumptions that a given group has invented, discovered, or developed in learning to cope with its problems of external adaption or internal integration."[3] The mission and vision are encapsulated in a short statement, intended to create unity and shared expectations, which can be transferred to the company's employees, suppliers, customers, and other stakeholders. Simply put, a company's mission, vision, and values seek to inspire employees, investors, customers, regulators, and suppliers by succinctly articulating what the company is and why it exists.

Many senior executives believe in the promise of their company's mission, vision, and values. Presumably, articulating them can inspire and culturally align employees, customers, suppliers, and other stakeholders. When asked about their company's strategy planning activities, many CEOs point to their mission, vision, and values workshop or retreat. In a typical workshop, a consultant encourages senior executives to come up with words and phrases that accurately capture their company's current and aspirational essence. They also ask the executives to describe how the words and phrases may inspire, and be interpreted by, different stakeholders. Through mutual discussions, the senior executives agree on a set of adjectives, nouns, and verbs they believe have inspirational value and describe their company's ethos.

For example, a leading business school paid a brand consultancy to help with a strategy embodied by the phrase "thought leadership." The school's mission and vision of thought leadership was intended to inspire its faculty to conduct high-quality research, students to lead with big ideas, and staff to support the ideas. Moreover, donors and supporters who valued the business school's preeminence in research leadership were expected to fund the school as it became a bastion of thought leadership. In terms of strategy, all activities and initiatives supporting thought leadership were to be prioritized and incentivized. Thus, the school would reward faculty for high-quality research and cutting-edge courses. It would, similarly, focus its communication strategy to reflect the new tagline of thought leadership. The school made it a priority to hold several conferences on its campus to promote its position as a thought leader. All in all, thought leadership was to become a fount of inspiration for all inputs (e.g., coursework, research, extracurricular activities, and communication) to promote outcomes such as student satisfaction, donations and philanthropy, a higher admissions rate, and improved school rankings.

The mission statement on insurance company Mutual of Omaha's website reads, "We will continue to build a corporate culture that respects and values the unique strengths and cultural differences of our associates, customers, and community." Marathon Oil Corporation's mission statement, also available on its corporate website, reads as follows: "Marathon is a company that strives to bring value and values together. We create value for our shareholders and provide quality products and services for our customers." Mission statements are intended to guide self-motivated employees to do their jobs and signal what is important and nonnegotiable to external stakeholders. Inspired by mission statements, employees are expected to more readily find a purpose and reason to coalesce around the companies' values. The promise of a mission, vision, and values statement rests in its ability to inspire and focus stakeholders to achieve the highest possible outcomes—real and aspirational—for an organization.

What are the perils of using a mission, vision, and values statement as a means for strategy? While the statements can be effective, they tend to be subjective and vague and have a broad, overarching scope. They rarely provide the focus and clarity needed to set strategy. For example, the business school abandoned its mission statement of thought leadership after several years. Many faculty members had no incentive to develop cutting-edge courses, as they could argue traditional courses promulgated thought leadership. Each conference and extracurricular activity was justified as providing thought leadership. Soon, the school was saddled with too many conferences, roundtables, and activities that displaced classroom activity. The school's research faculty size stagnated, while the staff size more than tripled. In other words, thought leadership became a conceptual umbrella to justify activities important to individuals within the business school. Leaders simply used the mission as an argument for their pet initiatives.

Most exercises around mission, vision, and values start as internal conversations about what the organization means to senior executives. The executive team attempts to ensure the mission, vision, and values also appeal to stakeholders like mid-level and frontline employees, customers, suppliers, and regulators. Executive teams explicitly focus their mission, vision, and values statements on the needs of stakeholders, providing resources that ultimately sustain the organization.

But starting with top management and extending out, the mission statements often become internally focused, then increasingly complex and abstract. For example, the business school's strategy consultants talked to faculty and staff, students, and potential donors (customers) to develop ideas for strategic positions the school could occupy. The positions were then incorporated in discussions and workshopped with senior members of the dean's office and board members, who crafted the thought leadership mission. Regardless of intent, senior management's professional ethos and aspirations ultimately drove the school's mission and vision. The organization became internally focused on senior management's needs, rather than customers' needs.

The more abstract a mission statement, the easier it is to justify as encapsulating the needs of different stakeholders. Yet, as mission and vision statements become more abstract, they are less likely to link to specific outcomes and hold stakeholders accountable. Few companies attempt to statistically link their mission, vision, and values to measures like profitability, sales growth, and margins. For the business school, students may articulate needs such as low tuition, a broad array of courses, flexible timing, a better job-placement office, and extensive career advice. Donors may have needs such as increased transparency and fund-use flexibility. However, each need may be deemed too specific to serve as a single and unifying vision. As such, senior executives and consultants rely on higher-level abstractions to define their mission and vision.

Abstract mission statements are open to multiple and competing interpretations.[4] Ultimately, they become difficult to implement and cannot be used to hold stakeholders accountable. The lack of accountability makes it difficult to deploy resources meaningfully. At the business school, the number of clubs, roundtables, conferences, and forums grew to more than 200 per year. The events cut into class time, created logistical difficulties for the planning team, and often led to sparsely attended events. The champion for each event was able to justify it in terms of building thought leadership, and the concept of thought leadership was inspiring to senior executives. But it failed to provide a robust template for allocating resources, holding employees accountable, and focusing effort. Moreover, the statement failed to provide guidance for competing priorities. Consider a faculty member being evaluated in terms of teaching and research. Which of the two areas contributes to thought leadership? Naturally, those excelling in research thought their activities contributed more to thought leadership than the activities of those excelling in teaching. Those excelling in teaching thought the opposite. When the school's dean created a weighting scheme to assess the relative contribution of teaching and research, many felt it was arbitrary, since no one knew how much teaching and research individually drove outcomes such as rankings, tuition, and student enrollment.

As one executive said in 2002, "Every last [mission statement] extols mom, apple pie, quality, and teamwork. Every last one of them is written in excruciatingly formal prose. And every last one of them, when reduced to essentials, simply states the obvious. What's really sad is that most of the newer mission statements are the products of the labors of some very smart executives ... So a lot of firms packed their most senior people off to expensive retreats to prepare this vital document ... And so, they worked very hard and then came home from the very expensive retreat with a brief document suitable for calligraphy ... And the document ... got tacked up on the wall and promptly forgotten ... The fact is, mission statements are rarely useful."[5]

A study conducted in 2020 analyzed 2000 CEOs' descriptions of their company's purpose. Incredibly, 93% failed to state why their company was in business, leading the study authors to conclude: "Most purpose statements lack any meaningful sense of purpose."[6] The assessment corresponds with the experience of Guardian Life Insurance Company, which offers life, health and disability insurance. According to MissionStatements.com, Guardian's mission states, "Our culture is based on an unwavering belief in integrity and fair dealings, treating our clients and each other with dignity and respect … We meet the needs of the markets we serve … We strive for excellence … We take prudent risks and work together to assure our success and profitability in the future … We work hard to enhance continuously our reputation for accessibility, professionalism, performance, and the depth and quality of our long-term consultative relationships with clients." While the values behind the statement are laudable, it is unclear which metrics are deployed to measure "striving for excellence." An all-encompassing pie-in-the-sky abstract mission statement makes it difficult to synthesize, manage, track, and disseminate critical metrics throughout an organization's hierarchy.

After its merger with a smaller competitor, abrasives and coatings firm ABCO (see Chap. 1 for a description) created a strategy around a new vision: "New abilities and new agilities to win." The vision sought to inspire employees to do everything possible to grow sales and margins. This meant 100% customer satisfaction, the best possible products and services, and outdoing competitors on product quality and customer service. ABCO told customers they could call the company for anything—products, service, expert advice, etc.—and consider it done. Senior executives assumed that, inspired by the ABCO mission statement, employees would be motivated to do everything possible for growing sales and margins.

The inspirational approach to strategy relies on a company's employees to deliver financial results. It is no wonder that ABCO, like many companies, made employee engagement the centerpiece of its strategy plan. But when surveyed about the strategy, only one of the company's 13 senior executives mentioned new abilities or agilities as critical. Instead, 80% of the senior executives listed three strategy priorities: operational efficiency, growth through acquisitions, and driving revenue. Only 50% of the executives agreed "differentiated and enhanced customer service" was a strategy objective. More startlingly, a systematic assessment of more than 200 customers showed they rated ABCO as average and no better than competitors on ongoing service and support. Despite its inspirational value to employees, the mission and vision statement failed to provide a meaningful mechanism to satisfy customer needs. Yet, management continued to believe that by engaging its employees to excel, ABCO would meet its strategic goals of growing sales and margins.

The assumption underlying an inspirational approach to strategy is that motivated employees can use their creativity and ingenuity to improve financial performance. Inspiring and motivating employees to draw the best out of them becomes the strategy's sole focus. Yet, a study of 135 companies showed that CEOs, senior executives, and consultants crafted the statement 72% of the times. Non-managers and middle managers participated in crafting mission statements 18% of the times and customers 2% of the times.[7]

4.2 Evaluating the Inspirational Approach to Strategy

One way to evaluate the inspirational approach to strategy is to consider research published in peer-reviewed scientific journals. Peer-reviewed research is based on diverse samples consisting of many companies, uses sound statistical techniques to isolate the unique association among variables of interest, and is free from the bias that creeps in when drawing conclusions based on a single company or a few executives.

The peer-reviewed studies examining the efficacy of mission, vision, and values statements in driving financial performance come in multiple forms. Some compare companies with mission, vision, and values statements to those without them. Others look at the content of the statements, evaluating whether certain terms correlate with financial performance. Notably, the studies include small and large companies, private and public companies, and businesses from all major continents. Thus, the results are robust and generalizable. Overall, the studies dispel the myth that strategy planning through mission, vision, and values improves a company's financial performance.

A 1989 peer-reviewed survey of BusinessWeek Global 1000 CEOs casts some initial doubt on the importance of mission statements.[8] Of the 181 CEOs surveyed, only 75 said their company prepared a formal mission statement. One reason CEOs said they did not develop a mission statement was to avoid answering the question, "What is our business?" The CEOs did not want to create conflict among senior executives over the basic purpose of the company. Moreover, the survey indicated companies did not use mission statements to develop actionable financial plans. For example, 83% of the statements included phrases associated with maintaining public image. Not a single firm reported a specific financial goal in its mission statement. In the words of the peer-reviewed study's authors, the statements were "generally declarations of attitude and outlook, rather than statements of specific programs of action."

Another study conducted in 1989 analyzed 59 companies in the Financial Times 1000 list.[9] The researchers found companies with mission statements were not more profitable than those without them. The study also found evidence most of the mission statements were internally focused. While 63% of the CEOs surveyed believed having a mission statement enabled better leadership and 53% believed it improved staff morale, 12% said it added no significant value. Only 16% said it attracted significant investment. Interestingly, the use of mission statements was no different among companies based on size, as measured by number of employees.

The results were replicated in another study, which considered 136 large Canadian organizations.[10] Researchers examined whether the presence or absence of a mission statement affected each company's return on assets. The results showed no difference in ROA between firms with or without mission statements. Indeed, companies with a mission statement appeared to have poorer profit growth than companies without one. No difference in ROA emerged between companies where CEOs felt satisfied versus dissatisfied with their mission statement. Specific mission statement elements, such as financial objectives, values, purpose, business strategy, and length, also showed no association with ROA.

A 1997 study surveyed 44 industrial CEOs and divided their mission statements into 25 components, ranging from values/philosophies to concerns for public image and stakeholders. The study found no relationship between the 25 mission components and average percentage change in sales and profits.[11] At best, the components were found to influence employee behavior.

A study conducted in 2006 analyzed the mission statements of 22 European, 15 Japanese, and 19 U.S. firms from the Fortune Global 500. It examined whether the statements included or excluded 17 specific variables, such as customers, investors, society, philosophy, financial objectives, sense of direction, competency, future orientation, and motivational phrases. The results showed no difference in ROA for companies using 14 of the 17 variables.[12] The authors concluded the inclusion of motivational appeal was not associated with higher financial performance but realized "motivational phrases in the mission statement might not be reinforced or aligned with operational goals, incentives, and rewards."

Other studies have shown similar results. A 2011 study sought to summarize existing strategy planning research using meta-analysis.[13] Meta-analysis is a statistical technique used in medical, social, and management science to quantify results across multiple independent studies.[14] Using statistical averaging, researchers summarize the results of all past studies to calculate the average effect size of a factor (e.g., use of mission statement) on an outcome (e.g., financial performance). The 2011 meta-analysis found a total of 14 studies with a combined sample size of 1945 units. Across the studies, the research team found the observed correlation between having a mission statement and financial performance was statistically no different than zero. In other words, despite the large sample across the 14 studies, the observed correlation of 0.23 was so small that it could have occurred by chance alone.

The available evidence from peer-reviewed studies debunks the notion that having a mission statement improves firms' financial performance. Companies with poor financial performance are no more or less likely to have a mission statement or specific mission statement elements than firms with high performance. Moreover, having a mission statement does not improve financial performance. Yet, some executives continue to believe developing mission statements is a critical part of strategy planning.

4.3   The Perils of Mission Statements

A cottage industry of brand strategists and consultancies has emerged to help companies write mission statements. Typically, the process involves the consultant (1) gathering information about the company's competitors, product/service line, and history; (2) talking to a few employees and customers; and (3) spending one to two days with senior executives.

Although it sounds straightforward, research shows that the process of writing a mission statement is fraught with roadblocks. Studies have documented many of the impediments, including managing the conflicting needs of diverse stakeholders, senior management's focus on operational issues, their disagreement over premises and assumptions, being too internally focused, an inability to link mission statements to execution priorities, and lack of a formal process for listening to and incorporating the priorities of key stakeholders.[15] The 2011 meta-analysis of mission statements showed that a majority, 64%, were static and half were internally focused on processes.[16]

For many companies, formulating a mission statement is a closed-door process. Senior executives, often facilitated by a consultant, formulate the statement and do nothing to test its effectiveness. Imagine a firm's executives and a consultant developing a brand and tagline without systematically testing alternatives through research with customers, employees, and suppliers. The company's likelihood of success would be almost entirely up to chance. The success of mission statements, produced in the same way, is likewise determined by chance alone. Studying the process of developing mission statements in 135 companies showed, "The top management group and the

CEO are most involved in creating the mission statement. Consultants are also involved. Despite the fact that the customer is the most frequently mentioned stakeholder in the mission statement, and that one of the more important uses of a mission statement is seen as ensuring that the interests of key external stakeholders (e.g., customers) are not ignored, the respondents in this study did not involve customers in the creation of their statements. This was recognized by some as unsatisfactory."[17]

Due to their abstract and broad nature, mission statements can overwhelm employees, who then sometimes harm their firm's bottom-line. For example, a mission statement including a phrase like, "providing excellent customer service," may offer employees leeway to reduce prices, increase promotional allowances, provide special handling, and give free gifts. Similarly, mission statements providing idealized or unattainable visions can frustrate employees. For example, a mission statement might suggest, "we will exceed customer expectations 100% of the time." One company's mission statement emphasized the value of "effective cash management." The vice president of finance therefore forced all vendors to accept late payments to maximize cash flow. Over time, high-quality vendors defected or held up supplies until they were paid in full, causing delays in customer deliveries, costing the company new business, decreasing morale among manufacturing plant employees, and causing supply chain headaches.

4.4   The Inspirational Approach: Research Evidence

To what extent do mission statements correspond with customer needs? In a December 2017 nationally representative online survey, 1001 oil and gas sector customers evaluated their suppliers. The suppliers were 50 of the most prominent energy sector companies: ExxonMobil, Shell, Schlumberger, Philips 66, Halliburton, National Oilwell Varco, and General Electric, to name a few. The proprietary survey measured the customers' overall satisfaction with the suppliers, along with eight strategic areas related to overall satisfaction. The strategic areas included initial sales and bidding, product and service quality, pricing and billing, communication, project management, safety, social responsibility and sustainability, and ongoing service and support.[18] The research statistically quantified the extent to which overall customer satisfaction responded to each strategic area. The response strength represented each area's relative importance. Strategic areas with higher relative importance were therefore more consequential in driving overall customer satisfaction, which drives sales, EBITDA, and margins.[19]

Was the relative importance of the eight strategic areas reflected in the mission statements of the 50 supplier companies? If a specific strategic area was present in the mission statement, it was considered salient (i.e., relatively prominent) to top management. If a strategic area was absent from a mission statement, it was considered less salient. A measure of salience was created by coding the 50 companies' mission statements for any mention of the eight strategic areas. The number of words referring to a strategic area was used to calculate the relative salience of each area for each firm. If a company's mission statement was completely based on customer needs, one would find a perfect positive correlation between strategic area salience and the statistical importance of each area, as derived from customer assessments. Yet, the correlation was a modest 0.20 and statistically no different than zero. In other words, the mission statements of 50 prominent energy sector suppliers were not at all associated with their customers' needs.

Figure 4.1 shows how the eight strategic areas' relative importance for customers corresponded with the areas' relative salience for the firms. The two measures diverged widely in some cases. While the energy companies' mission statements emphasized product and service quality, with a relative salience of 33%, the strategic area was not as important to customers, with a relative importance of 15%. Customers placed great importance on ongoing service and support (24%), but the firms' mission statements de-emphasized it, with a relative salience of 5%. Similarly, customers considered the area of initial sales/bidding important (12%), but mission statements gave it salience of

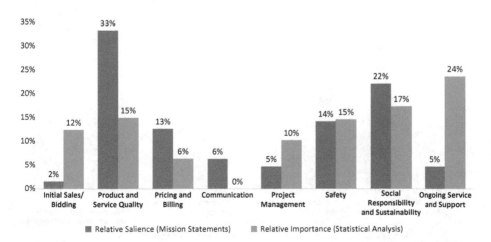

Fig. 4.1 Comparing strategic areas for energy companies using mission statements

only 2%. Overall, the evidence suggested companies' mission statements did not reflect their customers' needs, supporting the conclusion of earlier studies that the process of developing mission statements was inward-looking and ignored the needs of external stakeholders.

The conclusion can be further verified through the suppliers' 10-K statements. The statements are required by the U.S. Securities and Exchange commission and describe a company's history, goals, organizational structure, executive compensation, and other areas. Because they must comply with regulatory scrutiny, a company's 10-K report should guide and be guided by its mission statement, while being more detailed and more accurately reflective of executive intent. The same methodology used for analyzing the 50 energy sector companies' mission statements was applied to the 10-K statements. The study found a statistically significant correlation of 0.60 between the strategic areas' relative salience in mission statements and 10-K reports. The strong correlation suggests that senior executives emphasize the same strategic areas in their mission statements and 10-K reports. However, the correlation between the relative importance of the eight strategic areas to customers and their salience in the 10-K reports was –0.11. According to the 10-Ks, the 50 oil and gas sector companies failed to emphasize what their customers deemed important. Figure 4.2 shows how the relative importance of the eight strategic areas for customers corresponded with the relative salience of the eight strategic areas in the firms' 10-K reports. Several areas were widely divergent. For example, the energy companies' 10-Ks heavily emphasized pricing and billing (relative salience of 28%), but customers cared much less about it (relative importance of 6%). Customers considered ongoing service and

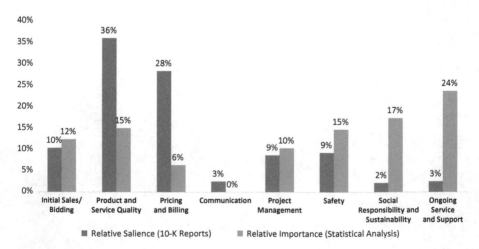

Fig. 4.2 Comparing strategic areas for energy companies using 10-K reports

support highly important (24%), but the 10-K reports mentioned it sporadically (relative salience of 3%).

Examining either mission statements or 10-K reports shows the mission, vision, and values approach to strategy planning tends to ignore the needs of external constituents like customers. The results are not unexpected—if the process of creating a strategic vision relies on consultants working with senior executives, issues salient to the executives are likely to be reflected in the outcome. While senior executives at some companies believe they "talk to customers," they do so in a manner inhibited by many biases (see Chaps. 7 and 8). The so-called customer feedback they receive consists of ill-structured, recall-based interviews lasting 30–90 minutes with handpicked customers. Research shows such interviews are statistically invalid and reflect the biases of the interviewer and interviewee. Interviewers ask questions salient to them, interviewees recite information readily available and salient to them, and the interviewers tend to agree with the interviewees, fueling confirmation bias.[20]

An examination of the mission statements of the top 100 U.S. B2B companies, based on annual revenue, showed a similar pattern. Companies on the list included Apple, AT&T, Bank of America, Berkshire Hathaway, ExxonMobil, Microsoft, Google, 3M, Dow, and Monsanto. Monthly surveys from a national panel of B2B managers from the top 100 companies, collected through 2017, measured the managers' overall satisfaction with their suppliers, as well as eight strategic areas related to overall satisfaction. As in the oil and gas study, the surveys were used to obtain the relative importance of the eight strategic areas in meeting customer needs and driving sales and margins. Relative importance was statistically calculated using a sample of 4105 surveys from 626 B2B customers. The financial performance data for each company evaluated in each survey was also obtained. The relative salience of the strategic areas of the top 100 B2B companies was taken from their mission statements.

The results highlighted the discrepancy between company mission statements and customer needs. As shown in Fig. 4.3, several areas were widely divergent. The B2B companies' mission statements emphasized quality, with a relative salience of 62%, but customers cared much less about it, giving it a relative importance of 19%. As in the oil and gas sector, customers emphasized ongoing service and support, giving it a relative importance of 33%, but the B2B companies' mission statements de-emphasized it, with a relative salience of 4%.

Using the B2B companies' 10-K reports to compare the relative salience of the eight strategic areas to their relative importance for customers, the gap persisted. As shown in Fig. 4.4, the companies' 10-K reports heavily

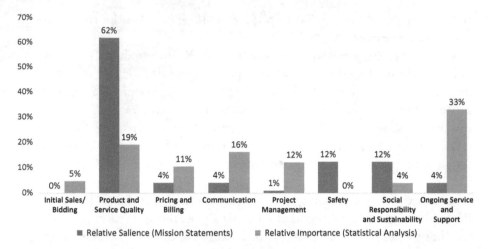

Fig. 4.3 Comparing strategic areas for B2B companies using mission statements

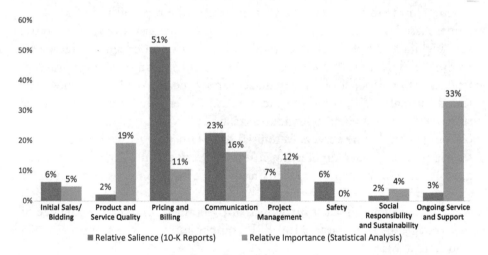

Fig. 4.4 Comparing strategic areas for B2B companies using 10-K reports

emphasized pricing and billing, with a relative salience of 51%, but customers cared much less about it, giving it a relative importance of 11%. Customers gave ongoing service and support a relative importance of 34%, but the firms' 10-K reports mentioned it less often than their mission statements, with a relative salience of 3%.

A weak correlation of 0.16 emerged between relative salience and customer importance in the top 100 B2B companies' mission statements. Statistically, the correlation was no different than zero, implying the statements were poorly connected to what was important to the firms' customers. The correlation between the relative importance of the eight strategic areas to customers and their salience in the B2B firms' 10-K reports was -0.07, statistically no different than zero. Contrary to the energy industry sample, a correlation of -0.28 emerged between the relative salience of the strategic areas in the B2B companies' mission statements and 10-K reports, indicating the statements and reports were not aligned.

Recall the FACILITYCO importance and salience results reported in Chap. 3, Table 3.3. The senior leaders' ranking of the eight areas presumably reflected their mission and vision for the company, with the highest ranking given to safety and sales/bidding. Yet the executives' designated importance in the eight areas was statistically uncorrelated with the importance customers placed on them. The same was true of ABCO and many other firms where executives relied on their own judgment to craft mission, vision, and values statements to guide strategy.

4.5 Conclusion

The inspirational approach to strategy planning is inwardly focused due to its heavy reliance on senior executives' input and bias-prone processes. Rather than focusing on the true needs of customers, executives using the inspirational approach focus on the issues they believe must be important to external stakeholders. The process becomes a feel-good exercise, devoid of rigorous data or analysis, and the resulting mission statements are unable to predict financial outcomes. In some cases, mission or vision statements can inspire employees to "do their best." But beyond broad, abstract, and vague directives, they do not clarify the specific activities and initiatives that help a company grow sales and margins.

Mission statements fare no better for strategy implementation. Despite some executives' strong belief in them, mission statements fail to provide employees focus, clarity, and accountability. They are overly general, broad, and vague, and employees can interpret them to suit their own needs, rather than the needs of critical stakeholders such as customers and shareholders. Mission statements also fail to provide the needed structure to implement and monitor specific initiatives that grow sales and margins. Importantly, mission statements fail to help employees prioritize initiatives and activities according to their impact on financial outcomes.

The existence or lack of a mission statement does not predict a company's financial performance. In medical terms, mission statements are no different than sugar pills or placebos. The lack of association between having a mission statement and superior financial performance refutes a strongly held belief in the strategy consulting community and among senior executives that mission or vision statements serve the interests of a financially accountable corporate strategy. If companies without a mission statement perform as well as companies with one, the conclusion is clear: rather than focusing on inspiring employees through mission and vision statements, senior executives—especially CEOs—should carefully consider the elements of strategy that make a difference.

Research systematically shows that mission statements ignore customer needs. Claims like "customers are important" or "we strive to serve our customers" do not account for specific needs. A quantitative analysis of mission statements in the oil and gas sector, as well as a wider B2B sector examination, confirms the intuition. Mission statements de-emphasize strategic areas important to customers, and not surprisingly, companies enamored with their mission statements often fail to meet customer needs. With their needs unmet, the customers are relatively unsatisfied, reducing sales and margins in the long run.

Notes

1. Mintzberg, Henry (1973), "Strategy-making in three modes," *California Management Review*, 16(2), 44–53.
2. Urde, Mats (2003), "Core value-based corporate brand building," *European Journal of Marketing*, 37(7/8), 1017–1040.
3. Schein, Edgar H. (1984), "Coming to a new awareness of organizational culture," *Sloan Management Review*, 25(2), 3–16.
4. Bartkus, Barbara, Myron Glassman, and R. Bruce McAfee (2000), "Mission statements: Are they smoke and mirrors," *Business Horizon, 43(6), 23–28.*
5. Mullane, John V. (2002), "The mission statement is a strategic tool: when used properly," *Management Decision*, 40(5), 448–455.
6. Michaelson, Christopher, Douglas A. Lepisto, and Michael G. Pratt (2020), "Why corporate purpose statements often miss their mark," *strategy+business*, August 17, 2020.
7. Baetz, Mark C. and Christopher K. Bart (1996), "Developing mission statements which work," *Long Range Planning*, 29(4), 526–533.
8. David, Fred R. (1989), "How companies define their mission," *Long Range Planning*, 22(1), 90–97.
9. Klemm, Mary, Stuart Sanderson, and George Luffman (1991), "Mission statements: Selling corporate values to employees," *Long Range Planning*, 24(3), 73–78.

10. Bart, Christopher K., and Mark Baetz (1998), "The relationship between mission statements and firm performance: An exploratory study," *The Journal of Management Studies*, 35(6), 823–853.
11. Bart, Christopher K. (1997), "Industrial firms and the power of mission," *Industrial Marketing Management*, 26(4), 371–383.
12. Bartkus, Barbara, Myron Glassman, and Bruce McAfee (2006), "Mission statement quality and financial performance," *European Management Journal*, 24(1), 86–94.
13. Desmidt, Sebastian, Anita Prinzie, and Adelien Decramer (2011), "Looking for the value of mission statements: a meta-analysis of 20 years of research," *Management Decision*, 49(3), 468–483.
14. Borenstein, Michael, Larry V. Hedges, Julian PT Higgins, and Hannah R. Rothstein (2011), *Introduction to meta-analysis*. John Wiley & Sons.
15. Ireland, R. Duane, and Michael A. Hitt (1992), "Mission statements: Importance, challenge, and recommendations for development," *Business Horizons*, 35(3), 34–42.
16. Desmidt, Sebastian, Anita Prinzie, and Adelien Decramer (2011), "Looking for the value of mission statements: a meta-analysis of 20 years of research," *Management Decision*, 49(3), 468–483.
17. Baetz, Mark C. and Christopher K. Bart (1996), "Developing mission statements which work," *Long Range Planning*, 29(4), 526–533.
18. Mittal, Vikas, and Shrihari Sridhar (2020), "Customer based execution and strategy: Enhancing the relevance & utilization of B2B scholarship in the C-suite," *Industrial Marketing Management*, 88(July), 396–409.
19. Collaborative for CUBES (2017), "Expanding margins: Collaborative for CUBES findings show right way to grow," CCUBES.net, CUBES Insight Series vol. 2.
20. Wallendorf, Melanie, and Merrie Brucks, (1993) "Introspection in consumer research: implementation and implications," *Journal of Consumer Research*, 20(3), 339–359.

5

The Superhero Executive: Strategy Planning Through Adhocracy

Who are superheroes? Superheroes are not beholden to rules. Superheroes take advantage of opportunities, solve problems, and achieve results against difficult odds. Superheroes are inventive, innovative, and creative. They tackle new challenges. Rather than waiting to be told what to do, superheroes figure out what needs to be done and act. They act even when the rules of engagement are unclear or do not exist, often deeming such rules restrictive. Superheroes take an informal, emergent, and unstructured approach to problem-solving that embodies an elevated level of risk-taking. Superheroes can achieve their goals alone, even when they do not have a broad set of colleagues, friends, and followers to support them.

Within organizations, superhero executives are exemplified by and symbolize the adhocratic approach to strategy planning.

An adhocracy is a type of informal organization that cuts across normal bureaucratic lines to capture opportunities, solve problems, and achieve results.[1] As an approach to strategy planning, adhocracy is informal, unstructured, and emergent. It embraces experimentation and improvisation. The first documented description of adhocracy as a strategy process examined the National Film Board of Canada, an organization devoted to artistic creativity and developing new products.[2]

An adhocratic approach to strategy views formal plans, roles, and processes as restrictive. Companies with an adhocratic bent embrace unplanned activities and view goals and processes as evolving over time, rather than being fixed. The adhocratic approach to strategy is often used in small businesses, startups, and new ventures. Creativity is seen as a key driver, and innovation and new products are critical to the company's success. Eschewing restrictive

V. Mittal, S. Sridhar, *Focus*, https://doi.org/10.1007/978-3-030-70720-0_5

rules and predefined roles—the hallmark of bureaucracy—senior executives in adhocratic organizations wear many hats. Each person might take on multiple roles and perform many functions and tasks on an as-needed basis. As such, the approach is also known as adaptive decision-making.[3]

Rather than having a predefined strategy, superheroes start with execution and adapt the strategy along the way. Similarly, adhocratic executives typically launch initiatives and use strategy to support the activities.[4] Consider Valve, a gaming firm in Bellevue, Washington. Rather than basing activities on a formal strategy plan with predefined objectives, processes, roles, and responsibilities,[5] Valve employees organize into self-selected teams around ideas or product opportunities. Billed as "boss-free since 1996," Valve avoids restrictive bureaucratic processes, formal project teams, and hierarchical management. Another large company embracing the adhocratic approach, U.K.-based pharmaceutical specialist Mundipharma, describes itself on its website as a global network of independent, associated companies focused on accelerating the development of meaningful medicines.

The adhocratic strategy planning approach is popular with many startups and small businesses where the owners operate the firms. The owner-operated business model is prevalent in professional services, such as physicians, accountants, contractors, insurance agents, food services, and property management. Observational studies spanning four years have uncovered a variety of adhocratic processes:

- A physician-owner of a medical practice focused on the daily activities of running the firm. Like a superhero, the owner undertook every challenge presented, whether daily, weekly, monthly, or quarterly. Bigger challenges representing long-term strategy goals, such as upgrading medical-records software, outsourcing billing, and adding new patient segments, were addressed on an ad hoc and as-needed basis. With action and day-to-day functions being primary, the physician made formal strategy planning a support activity.
- The president of a property management company focused on ensuring its 150 properties were fully rented and maintained. With a small staff of three employees, the team faced challenges such as plummeting occupancy rates during the COVID-19 pandemic, ensuring compliance with local laws, and appeasing property owners unable to collect rent due to tenant defaults. Keeping in mind the overall strategy goal of growing the properties under management, the team's daily activities focused on ensuring its owners and renters were satisfied. In the company's weekly planning meetings, the CEO often referred to the team as a band of superheroes. The company

sought to gain a competitive edge by improving its processes, such as using online software for rent deposits, outsourcing accounting, encouraging vendors to use online billing and payment, and using social media to gain customers. The innovations were undertaken on an ad hoc basis, prompted by specific customer demands. For example, a property owner asked for immediate evidence that repairs were done correctly before approving expenses. Rather than sending physical photographs, as in the past, the president took pictures using a cell phone, converted them to a single document, and posted them on a secure website. The digital process was adopted for every repair within weeks, lowering costs and increasing efficiency.

Just like the plot of a superhero movie, the adhocratic approach to strategy planning is fast-paced but sometimes chaotic. Its embrace of an informal, unstructured, and emergent approach acknowledges immediate critical tasks while improvising on long-term strategy goals. Still, the routineness of the emergent implementation tasks can provide a stable, consistent, and repeatable framework for identifying and meeting strategy goals. Thus, the medical practice aimed to serve a specific number of patients per week, while the property management company set goals to complete property repairs on time. The goals and targets not only were linked to daily implementation but also provided guidance and metrics to assess the organizations' strategy success. Adhocratic organizations simultaneously focus on completing day-to-day activities that create customer value, and addressing nonroutine challenges to innovate. Together, the two activities provide a framework for creating and implementing strategy.

Given their inherent flexibility, one would assume adhocracies have the potential to stay relevant for a long period. But as with superheroes, the promise of an adhocracy comes with perils. Adhocratic strategies seldom work for large organizations. Because they lack formal processes for detailed planning and assessment, adhocracies tend to be reactive rather than proactive. Bold plans to proactively and systematically seek change are scarce to nonexistent. Adhocratic organizations wrap themselves around their protagonist—the founder, the owner, the visionary—who is seen as a superhero by many employees. The organizations' success is tied to the abilities of their leaders, the protagonists, who can complete the routine tasks, address challenges, and use both activities to support strategy. In so many ways, employees and senior executives "leave it to the CEO" to drive company strategy. While the series of tasks seems chaotic and unrelated to outsiders and employees, it may clearly relate to and support the strategy in the CEO's mind. As Henry Mintzberg and colleagues stated, "In an organization in which all things—actions, decisions, projects, and especially the basic outputs—are so loosely coupled, in which management, hierarchy, and systems of control are so weak, it becomes fair to ask why patterning of behavior, namely strategy, appears at all."[6]

Due to a lack of clear strategy goals or process for setting goals, an adhocracy can become mired in political struggles. This is especially true when multiple protagonists are present or the visions of senior executives are misaligned. When multiple superheroes emerge, conflict is bound to occur, despite the best intentions. And in the absence of well-defined processes and policies, each protagonist charts a singular course, breeding conflict and eventually politicizing the adhocracy's strategy and execution.

Adhocratic strategy is laden with uncertainty, as it is meant to be fluid rather than stable and contract based. Employees in adhocratic organizations are seldom rewarded with long-term contracts smoothing their risk and are often coached to cope with transformational change.[7] Though having a strong protagonist in the form of an owner or founder can sometimes help sidestep political minefields, issues related to systematic goal setting and resource allocation persist. High uncertainty and a lack of goal-directed behavior within adhocratic organizations can exacerbate organizational conflict.

On the upside, the adhocratic approach emphasizes innovation, creativity, and agility. Like superheroes, adhocracies rely on speedy, high-risk, flexible innovation to respond quickly to market realities. The culture is entrepreneurial, adaptive and tuned to solving problems. Adhocracies generate new ideas faster than more staid and rigid organizations, transmit the knowledge and innovation with minimal bureaucracy, and capitalize on it. Like superheroes, adhocratic leaders in some ways simply "go at it" and let events unfold as they may. However, all aspects of the firm tend to rely on a loose coupling of processes, innovation spurts, and differentiation via products and services customers may not seek or need. The desire for the adhocracy's protagonist to be an explorer and hunter, while attractive, may not allow the company to settle, let ideas mature, solidify processes and structures, and gain stability.

5.1   Overemphasizing Exploration

Rigorous research published in peer-reviewed journals has examined adhocracies for more than two decades. The research typically classifies companies as having an exploration- or exploitation-based strategy,[8] where the processes represent two ends of a continuum. Exploration is adhocratic, espouses innovation, uses free-flowing processes, and is risky. Exploitation is systematic, espouses stability through repetitiveness, and is less risky. While exploration--based strategy processes (e.g., extensive R&D, developing new products, and channel expansion) reflect a discovery-orientation and flexibility, they are beset with inconsistency, uncertainty, and financial risk. Exploitation-based processes (e.g., incremental price increases for existing customers and the addition of products and services to a stable business) are about refinement and consistency and emphasize implementation maturity and execution consistency, rather than risky strokes of brilliance. For example, Google's CFO Ruth Porat helped transform the company from being exploration-based to being exploitation-based.[9] In its early years, Google was run by superheroes who emphasized innovation and experimentation at the expense of bureaucratic processes and budgetary controls. Market analysts raised red flags about the lack of financial controls and processes within the company's upper echelons. As a former Morgan Stanley executive who advised the U.S. government during the financial meltdown of 2008, Porat brought a more traditional approach to Google. As CFO, she introduced more controls and processes imposing financial discipline on the company's management practices. Moreover, with operations and human resources reporting directly to her, she was able to rein in Google's many superheroes.

Research shows balancing exploration and exploitation is optimal for driving financial performance. Firms need exploitative capabilities to compete in mature markets where cost and efficiency are critical, while being willing to explore new products and services to address new markets. A 2004 study of 206 manufacturing firms in Singapore and Malaysia showed simultaneously engaging in explorative and exploitative innovation strategies, termed ambidexterity, was important for driving sales growth.[10] Ambidextrous companies had a mean sales growth rate of 17.43%, nearly double the rate of purely explorative (8.59%) and exploitative (9.96%) firms. Over time, studies in several industries have supported the simultaneous need for exploration and exploitation, including in a[11]

- sample of 1073 analysts in 78 investment banks;
- multi-industry sample of 141 U.S. manufacturing firms;
- sample of 122 subject-matter experts in Chinese high-technology parks;
- study of 230 private firms in multiple industries; and
- sample of 716 managers at large firms.

Because adhocratic strategies tend to be heavily tilted toward exploration, they reduce ambidexterity and sales growth. A key reason is adhocratic strategies create organizational designs ill-equipped to deal with two funda-mental organizational challenges affecting strategy implementation:[12, 13]

(1) *Increasing interdependence while reducing coordination costs.* How con-nected are the inputs, processes, and outputs of each company function with those of other functions? When functions are highly interdependent, a company's coordination costs increase. For example, a B2B develop-ment team must consider on-time execution and cost when creating a project proposal. Therefore, the firm's project management function is likely interdependent with the development team. The unpredictability of adhocracies leads to new procedures to deal with coordination costs whenever they arise. In one adhocratic B2B company, the project man-agement team used separate spreadsheet templates to review proposals with every business development manager, increasing costs and creating inconsistencies. Ambidextrous organizations deal with coordination costs by standardizing repetitive processes. In another company, the project management team shared the same template with all business develop-ment personnel when discussing bids. The standardized process made implementation predictable while preserving creativity and adaptability among the project management and business development teams. The strategy also reduced coordination costs.

(2) *Increasing decision velocity while reducing uncertainty.* Modern firms must perform faster than ever before in their communications, new product development, human resource management, and on-time delivery. Increased velocity is attainable and beneficial only when companies can deal with uncertainty and keep costs down.[14] Dealing with uncertainty in a cost-effective way requires well-defined policies and processes. In the adhocratic B2B company mentioned previously, management consis-tently pressed the business development team to reduce lead times from reviewing requests for proposal to deciding whether to bid. The team needed to effectively deal with the ebb and flow of the project pipeline while having the ability to hire and fire personnel. But the team did not have strategy goals—or even the bases for setting them—nor design pro-cesses to deal with higher bid volumes. Eventually, the team became mired in politics, which debilitated the bid selection process. In another com-pany, which was ambidextrous rather than purely explorative, manage-ment created a rubric to make bid/no-bid decisions for each request for proposal received. The rubric was based on each project's size, region, scope, and fit and enabled the business development team to quickly determine if it was a potential win or loss. While bids somewhere between

a win and a loss had to be examined in detail, the process improved velocity by reducing the number of reviewed bids by up to 30%. The rubric allowed the company to discard losing bids, quickly submit bids on potential wins, and use the remaining time to consider other projects.

Adhocracies are ill-equipped to improve decision velocity in highly interdependent functions. The firms' protagonists can make all the decisions and make them quickly, but the process comes with high coordination costs and increased uncertainty. Outsiders and employees are unlikely to understand why and how the decisions are made. And they remain unsure how to implement the elected strategies. To understand and implement a decision properly requires clarity about strategy objectives, a plan to meet the objectives, and linking the objectives to financial outcomes valued by stakeholders. Ambidextrous companies are more capable than adhocratic or explorative companies to address the challenges.[15]

5.2   Overemphasizing Innovation

Adhocratic strategies emphasize exploration through innovation and creativity. Adhocratic protagonists expect their company's innovative products and services to drive sales growth and margins. The protagonists view sales growth as emanating from innovative and technologically advanced products that are new to the market and differentiate the company from competitors. It is not a coincidence that adhocracies are more prevalent among startups and small companies centered around specific products and services.

In academic research, an explorative emphasis is often measured via R&D spending. Scholars argue the investment signifies a company's willingness to innovate and take risks. A company's advertising budget is said to measure its exploitation tendency, as advertising is aimed at strengthening a brand among current customers, and ensuring stability. Typical studies have created an index of strategy orientation by subtracting a firm's relative R&D spending from its relative advertising spending. Higher scores signify higher exploitation or stability.

The strategy emphasis index can be linked to firm performance. A majority of studies have shown firms emphasizing exploitation over exploration have higher sales, better stock market performance, and lower stock market risk. For example:

- a 2002 study of 566 U.S. firms examined stock returns from 1980 to 1998 and showed emphasizing advertising over R&D increased stock returns;[16]
- a 2007 study of 644 U.S. firms examined data from 1979 to 2001 and showed emphasizing advertising decreased the idiosyncratic risk of company stock;[17] and
- a 2017 study of 2403 U.S. firms examined results from 2000 to 2014 and showed emphasizing advertising over R&D reduced the idiosyncratic risk of company stock.[18]

In each study, firms operating as risky adhocracies with a strategy focus on innovation did not outpace companies balancing innovation and stability. Thus, an adhocratic approach to strategy planning may provide sporadic anecdotes about effective superhero protagonists, but it does not lead to systematically superior financial performance.

5.3   Pioneering Industries

Another approach to understanding the relative success of adhocratic strategy planning is to examine industry pioneers, or "first movers." Adhocracies are widely associated with pioneering firms, the typical first mover in an industry that thrives on creativity and innovation. First movers tend to use adhocratic strategy approaches because their innovation has not yet been adopted, and they have no clear strategy goals or bases for setting goals.

A group of researchers conducted a meta-analysis of 90 studies measuring the relationship between order of market entry and performance. The studies covered many industry sectors (e.g., newspapers, semisubmersible oil drilling, and toothpaste) and countries (the United States, Canada, Norway, and Japan) and spanned more than 30 years.[19] The authors used market share and relative financial return (i.e., return on equity and return on investment) as performance measures. In each of the 90 studies, the authors coded whether the business unit was first to market, a pioneer, an early follower, or a late entrant. The ordinal scale captured the first-mover advantage in descending order. The study then related the first-mover measure to the two performance measures, market share and relative financial return. The researchers statistically removed the influence of extraneous factors, including industry competitiveness, which could have biased the effects downward, and industry survivability, which could have biased the effects upward. The study showed a positive association between the first-mover advantage and market share with 99% certainty. In other words, first movers consistently garnered higher market share. However, the researchers found zero association between the first-mover advantage and relative financial return. That is, the statistical association between the first-mover advantage and financial performance was no different than zero.

Another study compared the return on investment for industry pioneers and late market entrants.[20] The study statistically removed the biasing effect of firm-level and industry-level factors and concluded: "Pioneers in consumer goods industries had 3.78 [lower] ROI points than late entrants. In industrial goods, it was 4.24 points lower. Pioneers were substantially less profitable than followers over the long run, controlling for all other factors that could account for performance differences." Additional research by the same authors showed pioneers were at a substantial disadvantage on production rates and costs, eventually leading to decreased profitability.[21]

Adhocracy comes at a cost. The adhocratic approach to strategy planning may seem superhero-like, with supremely flexible leaders who experiment and improvise, take risks, and do not worry about tedious processes and procedures. But strategy flexibility increases uncertainty and coordination costs. Still, many senior executives run their companies as adhocracies, focusing on innovation, creativity, and R&D, and viewing stable processes, rules, and procedures as hindrances.

5.4   New Research

Many CEOs believe an adhocratic strategy is necessary for their companies to stay relevant, relentlessly innovate, and put out new products and services. Like the first documented adhocracy, the Film Board of Canada, most are focused on developing new products and services. The companies' CEOs and senior executives take pride in their innovation/R&D initiatives, establishing technology centers, rewarding employee patent production, focusing on digital initiatives to lower total ownership costs, and incentivizing employees to develop new product ideas. Many adhocratic companies celebrate their vitality index, defined as new product revenues as a percentage of total revenues. A common refrain among senior executives is that their "customers demand innovative products," with product innovation becoming the sine qua non of their strategies. But how much do customers really care about new products, technology, and innovation?

Recall the national survey of 626 B2B companies' customers covering a variety of industries, jobs, rank, and experience. The 4105 survey respondents rated their overall satisfaction with vendors from industries like manufacturing, services, information technology, office supplies, chemicals, banking, and distribution, to name a few. Each respondent rated overall satisfaction and satisfaction with eight strategy areas related to overall satisfaction. The eight areas were initial sales and bidding, product and service quality, pricing and billing, communication, project management, safety, social responsibility and sustainability, and ongoing service and support. Innovation investments should have their greatest effect on the strategy area of product and service quality. Therefore, if the underlying strategy goal of adhocracies is effective, product and service quality should be the dominant customer value driver.

Figure 5.1 shows the relative importance of the eight strategy areas in driving overall customer value. Customers gave product and service quality 19% weight. Overemphasizing product or service quality at the expense of other strategy areas, which accounted for the remaining 81% of customer value, appeared to be a mistake. Customers gave 33% weight to ongoing service and support, which emerged as the most important strategy area driving overall customer value. Research conducted on behalf of other companies has shown the same pattern. Ongoing service and support, communications, and project management typically account for more than 50% of overall customer value. Companies emphasizing product innovation at the expense of reliable and high-quality customer support, communication, and project management are unlikely to optimize value for their customers.

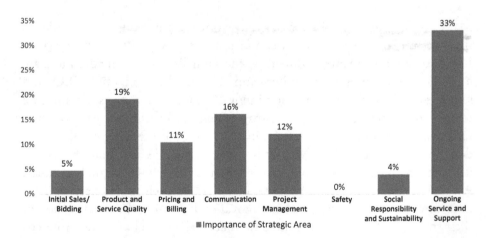

Fig. 5.1 How eight strategic areas drive B2B customer value

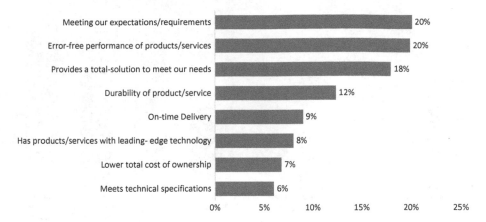

Fig. 5.2 How execution levers enhance product/service quality for B2B customers

Drilling further into product and service quality can better identify the weight of specific execution levers driving the strategy area (see Fig. 5.2). Execution levers with a higher weight are considered more influential in driving product and service quality performance for customers. Figure 5.2 shows the relative weight and performance of specific execution levers associated with the strategy area. Customers cared most about the product/service meeting expectations and requirements (20% weight), providing error-free performance (20% weight), and offering a total solution to meet their needs (18% weight). They placed an 8% weight on leading-edge technology. So a company wanting to enhance overall customer value through product and service quality should focus on meeting requirements and error-free performance, rather than on leading-edge technology. What was the total impact of having leading-edge technology as traced through product and service quality? A meager 1.5% (8% × 19%). Companies using an adhocratic approach may emphasize R&D and innovation in the interest of technologically superior products. But in the study, products with the latest technology accounted for less than 2% of customer value. If a company's entire strategy is driven by a lever responsible for less than 6% of the value it provides, what are the odds the strategy successfully delivers sales growth?

The analysis can be repeated with data from the December 2017 energy benchmark study, which captured a nationally representative online survey of 1001 customers in the oil and gas sector. Figure 5.3 shows how the relative

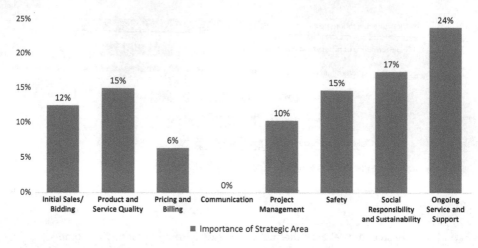

Fig. 5.3 How eight strategic areas drive value for energy customers

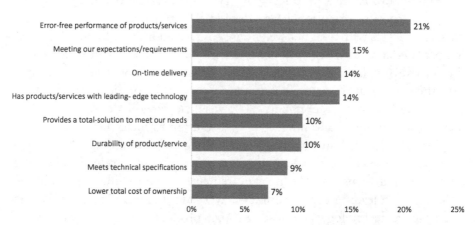

Fig. 5.4 How execution levers enhance product/service quality for energy customers

importance of the eight strategy areas drove customer value. The benchmark study participants gave product and service quality 15% weight in driving value. Drilling down into product and service quality to better identify the weight of specific execution levers shows an interesting pattern (see Fig. 5.4). Customers cared most about the products and services offering error-free performance (21% weight) and leading-edge technology (14% weight). They weighted meeting technical specifications at 9%. The total weight of leading-edge technology in satisfying customer value was only 2.1% (15% × 14%).

5.5   Conclusion

Adhocratic strategy planning processes, which tend to favor exploration over exploitation, often induce a strategy imbalance and satisfy 2%–6% of customer needs. Thus, they offer limited ability to generate cash flow through sales growth. Of course, the extent to which innovative products drive customer value and sales growth remains an open question.

From a strategy perspective, adhocracies can tilt a company toward unending experimentation and R&D, at the expense of meeting basic customer needs. In terms of implementation, the lack of defined processes and policies in adhocracies can increase coordination costs, inflate the risk of project failure, and create conflict and political infighting. Due to an overreliance on superhero protagonists, employees may lack the initiative to create or implement strategy. From a financial perspective, an overemphasis on adhocratic strategy can put companies on a path of profligacy, increasing the risk of failure and leaving customers unsatisfied. Indeed, it was a pattern of adhocratic behavior that Ruth Porat stemmed at Google, cutting spending on moonshot divisions, promoting austerity and discipline, and leading to a quantum leap in the company's stock price.[22]

Despite the promise of adventure, risk seeking, novelty, and creativity, an adhocratic approach to strategy can be perilous for any company.

Notes

1. Waterman, Robert H. (1990), *Adhocracy*. W.W. Norton & Company.
2. Mintzberg, Henry, and Alexandra McHugh (1985), "Strategy formation in an adhocracy," *Administrative Science Quarterly*, 30(2), June, 160–197.
3. Mintzberg, Henry (1973), "Strategy-making in three modes," *California Management Review*, 16(2), 44–53.
4. Birkinshaw, Julian, and Jonas Ridderstråle (2015), "Adhocracy for an agile age," *McKinsey.com*, December.
5. Valve website. https://www.valvesoftware.com/en/people
6. Mintzberg, Henry, and Alexandra McHugh (1985), "Strategy formation in an adhocracy," *Administrative Science Quarterly*, 30(2), June, 160–197.

7. Schimmoeller, Leon J. (2010), "Leadership styles in competing organizational cultures," *Leadership Review*, 10(2), 125–141.

8. March, James G. (1991), "Exploration and exploitation in organizational learning," *Organization Science*, 2(1), 71–87.

9. Rao, Leena (2016), "The Wall Street veteran who's helping Google get disciplined," *Fortune.com*, September 12.

10. He, Zi-Lin, and Poh-Kam Wong (2004), "Exploration vs. exploitation: An empirical test of the ambidexterity hypothesis," *Organization Science*, 15(4), 481–494.

11. Raisch, Sebastian, Julian Birkinshaw, Gilbert Probst, and Michael L. Tushman (2009), "Organizational ambidexterity: Balancing exploitation and exploration for sustained performance," *Organization Science*, 20(4), 685–695.

12. Parikh, Margie (2016), "Move over Mintzberg, let adhocracy give way to ambidexterity," *Management Decision*, 54(5), 1047–1058.

13. Child, John, and Rita Gunther McGrath (2001), "Organizations unfettered: organizational form in an information-intensive economy," *Academy of Management Journal*, 44(6), 1135–1148.

14. Eisenhardt, Kathleen M. (1989), "Making fast strategic decisions in high-velocity environments," *Academy of Management Journal*, 32(3), 543–576.

15. Parikh, Margie (2016), "Move over Mintzberg, let adhocracy give way to ambidexterity," *Management Decision*, 54(5), 1047–1058.

16. Mizik, Natalie, and Robert Jacobson (2003), "Trading off between value creation and value appropriation: The financial implications of shifts in strategic emphasis," *Journal of Marketing*, 67(1), 63–76.

17. McAlister, Leigh, Raji Srinivasan, and MinChung Kim (2007), "Advertising, research and development, and systematic risk of the firm," *Journal of Marketing*, 71(1), 335–348.

18. Han, Kyuhong, Vikas Mittal, and Yan Zhang (2017), "Relative strategic emphasis and firm-idiosyncratic risk: The moderating role of relative performance and demand instability," *Journal of Marketing*, 81(4), 25–44.

19. VanderWerf, Pieter A., and John F. Mahon (1997), "Meta-analysis of the impact of research methods on findings of first-mover advantage," *Management Science*, 43(11), 1510–1519.

20. Boulding, William, and Markus Christen (2008), "Disentangling pioneering cost advantages and disadvantages," *Marketing Science*, 27(4), 699–716.
21. Boulding, William, and Markus Christen (2001), "First-mover disadvantage," *Harvard Business Review*, 79(9), 20–21.
22. Chafkin, Max, and Mark Bergen (2016), "Google makes so much money, it never had to worry about financial discipline—until now," *Bloomberg.com*, December 8.

6

The Analytical Executive: Budget-Based Strategy Planning

A budget-based strategy planning approach emphasizes formal and systematic processes to obtain information, coupled with budgeting, to set goals, allocate resources, and hold employees accountable for key performance indicators. It is also known as the corporate-planning approach, because the majority of planning activities rely on the corporate budget for resource allocation. The budget-based or corporate-planning approach assumes financial budgeting sets strategy by focusing resources and driving accountability and alignment throughout a company. Most medium-sized to large organizations in traditional manufacturing and service sectors use the budget-based strategy planning approach.

The budget-based approach is based on three precepts: (1) systematic planning is anticipatory and done in advance of taking action, (2) planning is required and necessary when the future is predicated on interdependent decisions involving multiple actors, and (3) planning is required when specific actions can produce desired future states.[1] The budget-based strategy planning approach was used by early proponents of quantitative disciplines like operations research, economics, accounting, and finance. The goal was to develop plans to simultaneously optimize multiple operational aims and produce desirable financial outcomes (e.g., manufacturing efficiencies contributing to margins).[2] The strategy rose to prominence as quantitative disciplines became increasingly ingrained in management thinking.

The budget-based strategy planning approach is heavily integrated with financial budgeting. Whether done annually or at other intervals, a typical budget-based strategy planning approach is intertwined with a desire to balance operational excellence and financial control. A firm's functional groups

V. Mittal, S. Sridhar, *Focus*, https://doi.org/10.1007/978-3-030-70720-0_6

set operational targets and objectives and carefully budget the associated resources to control employee activities. Over time, the firms hold personnel accountable for results based on budgetary achievements (e.g., sales, cash flow, or cost savings).

A typical budget-based planning cycle starts with the CFO setting financial goals, such as revenue or sales growth targets, in consultation with the CEO. Different departments and divisions then use these goals to plan their activities. For example, facilities management, catering, and support firm FACILITYCO (see Chap. 1 for a full description) had sales of $1.5 billion. In consultation with the board, the CEO set a goal to increase sales by 8%, or $120 million, over three years. The CFO then worked with each department to develop budget-based plans for reaching the target. The sales group created a plan and accompanying budget to increase the number of leads and bids submitted by 50%. The group hired additional sales team members for lead generation, expanded its proposal writing group, and streamlined follow-up on each submitted proposal. The sales department estimated an increase of $2.1 million in its annual budget but assured management it would close an additional $50 million in sales. The assurance was based on a detailed strategy for approaching a certain number of prospects and converting them into successful bids. Other departments provided similar plans and justified an increase in expenses based on a projected contribution to sales.

Most budget-based strategy plans aim to increase overall revenues or margins. From there, each department, division, or group creates a plan and budget allocated to various initiatives and execution levers. The initiatives and levers are directly or indirectly linked to an increase in the overall strategy goal of sales or margin growth. A budget-based approach to strategy planning conceives a reality where financial goals can be met by incentivizing critical behaviors and allocating resources to key initiatives. Thus, a CEO might decide generating leads is a critical behavior and increase the sales team budget. Budget-based CEOs and CFOs, along with their division heads, use their best judgment in deciding which behaviors and initiatives are critical and which are not.

Many CEOs and CFOs find the budget-based approach to strategy planning intuitively appealing. It enables a CEO to set concrete goals, allocate budget in a measurable way, and use income and cash flow statements to monitor progress. Two examples are as follows:

- A small manufacturing company with $50 million in annual sales operated primarily in Europe (92% of sales), with a small office in the United States. It set a strategy goal to expand its U.S. presence and increase sales by 30%

or $15 million in three years. Its three operational objectives included hiring a full-time business development professional, upgrading the U.S. facility to include destructive parts testing, and acquiring another company for $5 million to $10 million. The vice president directing the expansion developed a budget requiring an investment of $250,000 in year one and $400,000 in year two, in addition to obtaining a line of credit. The vice president developed sales projections and set operational targets for each of the strategy goals. The firm gave its human resources director a timeline for hiring the business development professional, discussed acquisition targets with private equity companies, and presented a business plan to banks that could provide the line of credit. Senior executives believed business development through a local office would be the main sales growth driver.

• Executives at an engineering and construction company with $6 billion in annual sales examined the firm's budget and concluded they needed to improve profitability. They said it was "what our shareholders are expecting from us." The executives asked each division to develop a plan for increasing sales and EBITDA by 5% over the previous year. The largest division focused on several strategy initiatives related to efficiency—innovation through digitization, outsourcing low-value-added services, and reviewing low-margin businesses for divestment. Each initiative's sponsor strongly believed their effort was highly correlated with sales and margin growth. A technical sales director was put in charge of developing a digital initiative. The human resources director was selected to head the outsourcing initiative. And the division president and senior vice president of sales reviewed divestment candidates. The sales director argued digitization would create switching costs for customers, who would be locked into buying the company's monitoring service. The effort would not only increase sales, but also lower costs, resulting in expanded margins. The HR director was convinced outsourcing customer service would result in cost savings with a negligible effect on sales. The executive team developed detailed projections for initial costs, potential savings, and EBITDA changes to navigate the strategy planning process. Working with the finance and accounting group, the executives developed detailed budgets associated with each initiative and integrated them into the company's larger plan. The net result was a decrease in profitability. The digital initiatives required an upfront investment of more than $10 million, the outsourcing initiative required layoff packages and long-term supplier contracts of $3 million, and the low-margin business divestment required a write-down of more than $50 million. The underlying logic for why each initiative would grow EBITDA by expanding sales and lowering costs—airtight for each champion—did not hold up.

6.1 Evaluating the Budget-Based Approach

Why is the budget-based approach to strategy planning prevalent at large companies? Interviews with CEOs and senior leaders provide clues. Aside from the ability to hold employees accountable through budgetary control mechanisms, a budget-based approach provides senior management a clean slate to test their hypotheses about strategy success. For example, a CEO who truly believes financial success is a consequence of highly engaged employees can support the belief by allocating additional budget for initiatives supporting engagement. The initiatives may include employee training, culture building, or improved benefits. If an increased budget for employee training leads to improved financial performance, the CEO's belief in engagement is validated. CEOs also prefer the budget-based approach because it is easy to communicate to their board, as well as outside stakeholders like financial analysts. To the extent that boards and stock analysts may be focused on financial outcomes, the budget-based approach makes it easier to communicate initiatives, goals, and activities.

One study demonstrated the appeal of the budget-based approach by examining three organizations: a bureaucratic public service group, a large city hospital, and an art production house.[3] The study concluded the perceived benefits of formal budget-based strategy planning manifested in four outcomes:

1. *Group therapy.* The organizations' senior executives viewed the budget-based strategy planning approach as a way to obtain input and commitment from all levels, while providing a structured platform for their strategy goals and vision. It "brought people on board" by making them feel important, educated, and legitimately involved in the planning process. Done properly, the approach served to communicate the three management groups' strategy goals and motivate employees to implement them. The communication process was facilitated by using budget statements, which senior leaders and division heads clearly understood. The approach sought to build cohesion and consensus about the organizations' strategy goals among stakeholders.

2. *Public relations.* The budget-based approach communicated senior executives' action plans to external stakeholders. In the three organizations, leaders and employees said they saw the plans as tools to "impress outsiders." According to the study authors, public sector companies often use the planning process as a public relations strategy. In the private sector, subsid-

iaries see the strategy plan as a way to affirm their commitment to their parent firm.[4] Not surprisingly, analyst calls with public firms and CEO meetings at private equity groups often focus on budgetary elements.

3. *Information.* The three organizations' budget-based approaches provided a pretext to gather, exchange, and morph information into a common format, especially when CEOs were new. CEOs dove into the organizations' budgets and other documents, using spending patterns and monetary allocation to learn about them. The organizations saw the information gathering process as a way to learn, generate knowledge, and cull insights. Problems with the approach surfaced when mid-level and frontline employees viewed it with skepticism. Some believed senior executives used the budget-based strategy planning approach to gather and disseminate conforming information to verify and support their preset goals, ideas, and agenda.

4. *Direction and control.* The budget-based approach was used by some organizations to create alignment and ensure they focused on strategy priorities. Senior executives emphasized or de-emphasized goals, activities, departments, or initiatives by increasing or decreasing their budget. The individuals charged with developing each focus were empowered with significant decision-making authority. For such organizations, strategy planning also helped create specific goals, processes, and metrics to monitor progress and drive accountability within subdivisions. The groups did not achieve their goals when executives used the process to gain clout or "favorable prejudice" over their own divisions, which sometimes led to misaligned incentives. Unless the incentives were fully aligned, executives often created confusing "priority initiatives" that led frontline employees in different directions.

Does the budget-based approach achieve its objectives and improve financial performance? A number of researchers have considered the question. A 1976 study identified 2000 companies using or planning to use a budget-based strategy process.[5] The authors surveyed senior executives in the companies and received 346 responses:

- The typical corporate-planning or budget-based approach users were the companies' vice presidents of finance (55%) and presidents (46%). The firms' chairpersons (23%) and vice presidents of marketing (29%) were least likely to use budget-based planning.
- Large firms were more likely to use the corporate-planning or budget-based approach. Firms with annual sales of $500 million to $1 billion (21%) and

$1 billion or more (38%) were most likely to use the process. Firms with annual sales of less than $50 million (7%) and $50 million to $100 million (3%) were least likely to use it.

- What was the motivation to use budget-based strategy planning? Most companies wanted to evaluate policy alternatives (79%), create financial projections (75%), and plan for the long term (73%). Analysis (39%), confirmation of analysis (35%), and corporate goal setting (46%) were the least cited motivations.
- The most prominent corporate-planning outputs included cash flow analysis (65%), balance sheet projections (65%), and financial analysis (64%). Short-term forecasts (33%), marketing planning (33%), and investment analysis (35%) were the least common applications.
- How often was budget-based planning done? It was akin to a hunch or craving. Most corporate-planning activities occurred "when necessary" (33%).

Senior managers participating in the 1976 survey also highlighted budget-based planning's limitations. Among respondents, 25% believed it was not flexible enough, 23% believed it was poorly documented, and 23% believed it needed too much data for decision-making.

A 2014–2015 survey of 145 chief financial officers in Asian countries showed even more striking results.[6] When asked about the importance of skills needed to be an effective CFO, 58% said strategy planning and 52% said people management. Only 42% rated commercial acumen as the most important skill for a CFO. The findings were consistent with the results of a *McKinsey Quarterly* survey conducted among 796 managers worldwide.[7] The survey showed a surprising level of disillusionment, dissatisfaction, and disagreement among respondents about the strategy planning process. Only 64% believed strategy planning led to decisions allowing a company to meet its challenges and goals. Only 57% believed the strategy planning process was fact-based, and 53% believed it actually focused on strategy issues and not tactical issues. Most telling, only 35% of participants felt they received worthwhile analyses and information at the right time in the strategy planning process, leading 20% to believe the process was efficient.

How, when, and why can budget-based planning create value for companies? A study conducted in 1983 sought to examine corporate characteristics that eroded value (i.e., in companies with low ROI).[8] The study was among the first research projects to leverage the Marketing Science Institute's Profit Impact of Marketing Studies (PIMS) data. Originally built in the 1970s, the PIMS database contained specific and objective metrics allowing researchers to identify how strategies could be associated with performance. The database was built from GE's 1960s-era corporate management models, which used a range of strategy factors to optimize firm performance. PIMS tracked self-reported competitive strategies, including firms' relative price, quality, direct costs, marketing expenditures, geographic expansion, and supplier concentration. In addition to the PIMS data, the 1983 study measured firmographic variables, such as industry group, business type, and age. Because the study merged financial and PIMS data, it allowed a unique and clear window into specific strategies pursued by companies and their impact on financial outcomes.

The study defined low ROI market leaders as those with pre-tax ROI of less than 10% and a change in market share of less than 3% between 1972 and 1975. High ROI market leaders had a pre-tax ROI of greater than 40% and change in market share of more than 3% between 1972 and 1975. What differentiated low ROI and high ROI market leaders? The study found:[9]

- Low ROI companies had a 24% chance of confronting 20 or more competitors in their market, while high ROI companies had an 8% chance. Similarly, 24% of the low ROI companies operated in regional markets, while 8% of the high ROI firms did so. Low ROI companies appeared to disadvantage themselves by picking regional and competitively crowded markets.
- While only 20% of the high ROI companies emphasized raw or semi-finished materials and de-emphasized auxiliary services, 44% of low ROI companies said auxiliary services were important for generating demand. High ROI companies appeared to be more focused on core offerings.
- 61% of low ROI companies, but only 34% of high ROI companies, sought the services of professional advisers.

What aspects of competitive strategy differentiated the low ROI and high ROI leaders?

- Low ROI companies had a 7% price premium on average, while high ROI firms had a 4% premium. Price premium alone did not guarantee profitability.
- High ROI companies earned a relative quality score of 48 (measured as the difference between the firm's percentage of superior and inferior goods), while low ROI companies had a relative quality score of 31.
- High ROI companies had 98% of the direct costs of their competitors, while low ROI companies had 105% of competitor costs.

High ROI companies had lower costs, better quality, more focused offerings, and a more competitive price point. At the same time, they were less reliant on consultants for strategy advice. Though the study authors did not quantify other factors, they stated low ROI companies spent less on marketing activities, were more vertically integrated, and tended to be less standardized than high ROI firms. It therefore appeared no magic formula separated the characteristics eroding value. Moreover, it was unlikely that an emphasis on low costs via efficiency—a major emphasis of budget-based strategy planning—guaranteed profitability.

Using a corporate-planning approach or budget-based strategy planning process may lead firms to pursue goals that are unrelated, poorly related, or even negatively related to financial performance. A 1994 study examined financial performance by comparing firms using one of four formal strategy planning approaches to firms using no formal planning.[10] The study measured financial performance using return on capital for the following five groups:

- *Corporate strategy planners.* Firms making strategy plans at the corporate and division levels, with divisional plans being integrated into the corporate plan.
- *Division strategy planners.* Firms making strategy plans at a division level but not integrating them into a corporate plan.
- *Corporate financial planners.* Firms making financial but not strategy plans at the corporate level by projecting trends and making budgets.
- *Divisional financial planners.* Firms making financial but not strategy plans at only the division level by projecting trends and making budgets.
- *Non-planners.* Firms not making strategy or financial plans at any level.

The study[11] found that non-planners exhibited a higher return on capital (13.2%) than any of the four strategy planning groups (9.2%–12.0%). Engaging in corporate planning did not ensure success. Among the four planning groups, corporate strategy planners exhibited the highest return on capital (12.0%), followed by divisional strategy planners (11.0%), corporate financial planners (10.5%), and divisional financial planners (9.2%). Simply incorporating budgeting and forecasting was therefore inferior to developing strategy priorities.

The study[12] found that non-planners in the sample exhibited a lower chance of long-term survival (an average 15-year survival rate of 29%) than any of the four planning groups (39%–70% survival rate). Engaging in corporate planning may have mitigated bankruptcy risk. Division strategy planners exhibited the highest 15-year survival rate (70%), followed by corporate strategy planners (67%). Divisional financial planners (55%) and corporate financial planners (39%) had dramatically lower survival rates. For a firm's survival, incorporating budgeting and forecasting in strategy planning did not provide insurance. The process needed to be combined with strategy priorities implemented at all company levels.

The evidence has shown that budget-oriented strategy planning tends to make firms more inward looking, with a heightened focus on financial metrics. A budget-based planning process emphasizes activities managers believe are directly linked to financial metrics, the major yardstick for measuring success. The process therefore focuses all personnel attention on activities concretely and directly linked to measures like costs or revenues. Although corporate goals are framed in terms of sales growth, budget-based plans often lack any explicit mechanism to statistically determine the relative impact of budget allocation on sales. Rather, initiative proponents assume their projects are associated with certain financial outcomes.

Budget-based plans put a premium on cost cutting and efficiency boosting. Activities such as new product development, mergers and acquisitions, and R&D are often emphasized and justified because they increase sales. Activities directly benefitting customers—restrained price increases, additional service and support, and being customer-focused—are more difficult to link to revenues. Therefore, a budget-based approach may short-circuit customer needs, which are less tangible and more distal from the budget allocated to internal initiatives.

Firms using budget-based strategy planning often focus on activities where a tangible, upfront outlay is expected to have a direct link to increased sales or reduced costs. For example, most new product investments require an upfront research and development outlay, and the new and/or superior product is expected to generate sales. Thus, if senior executives believe new products with superior technology drive sales, they allocate more budget to product development. In many companies, mergers and acquisitions are justified on the basis of reducing costs through shared corporate services and increasing sales via new products and markets. Coatings and abrasives firm ABCO's budget-based strategy, for example, relied on acquiring competitors.

Budget-based planners often justify operational-excellence initiatives in terms of cost reductions because they expect them to expand margins. A budget-based approach does not provide senior executives with a way to determine if the cost cutting could harm the organization in other ways, such as letting go of experienced employees who may be hired by competitors or reducing the company's ability to satisfy customers. Worse, attempts to directly link firm activities to outcomes like sales and margins tend to bypass the customer.

Consider Wells Fargo, which was fined $185 million in 2016 for opening roughly 1.5 million bank accounts and applying for 565,000 credit cards not authorized by customers.[13] The bank's strategy plan and employee incentives were based on cross-selling, or increasing sales to existing customers by delivering more products. The approach to increasing sales did not meet customer needs but bypassed them entirely. According to the *New York Times*, Wells Fargo gave one customer seven accounts without consent. The customer suffered from a reduced credit score because of unpaid fees. On the surface, Wells Fargo's cross-selling approach created value, emphasized by a strategy plan explicitly rewarding the practice. As reported in 2017, "the word 'cross-sell' appeared five times in Wells Fargo's earnings report. The bank mentioned it eight more times in a presentation to Wall Street. The key message Wells Fargo wanted to drive home to its shareholders: The bank averaged an impressive 6.1 products per household, far better than the rest of the industry."[14]

Like many companies relying on budget-based strategy, Wells Fargo's plan emphasized internal activities directly affecting revenues, with less regard to their impact on customer value. Even as the scandal unfolded, Wells Fargo planned to cut about $2 billion in annual expenses by the end of 2018 and close 200 branches. By 2020, Wells Fargo's stock lagged its competitors, such as Bank of America and JPMorgan Chase, and its most ardent and largest investor, Warren Buffet, had sold the majority of his stake in the firm.[15]

The General Electric saga further illustrates the point.[16] Under Jack Welch, General Electric maintained a strong customer focus. "Marketing isn't somebody's responsibility," he famously said. "Marketing is everybody's responsibility." But as the company became more inwardly focused under Jeff Immelt, its strategy relied increasingly on financial engineering and acquisitions designed to add revenue or lower costs. The company's stock careened downward, but Immelt argued its business was booming and investors had mispriced it. As General Electric's customer base faltered and the company lost lucrative service contracts in late 2018, one oil and gas division director confessed in a personal communication, "We just became too internally focused and lost touch with our customers."

For firms using budget-based strategy plans, bolt-on acquisitions are seen as a way of increasing revenues, even when they ignore customer needs. Similarly, letting go of employees is seen as a cost reduction strategy, even as it negatively impacts customers. Invariably, the companies become more inwardly focused. Senior executives focus on analyzing every internal activity and justifying each as a driver of increased revenues or decreased costs. It is not surprising the biggest proponent of budget-based strategy planning is typically a firm's CFO or COO. But due to its reliance on budgeting, the approach detracts from strategy elements like satisfying customer needs.[17]

As GE and Wells Fargo illustrate, increasing sales and cutting costs without satisfying customer needs should not be confused with satisfying customers to increase sales and margins. The former is a widespread practice underlying budget-based strategy planning. The latter is not. After all, budget-based strategy planning is oriented toward optimizing the internal workings of a company, whether cutting costs or implementing initiatives. Rarely does the process correlate a budgeting decision to its impact on employee or customer satisfaction.

6.2 Examining New Evidence

The budget-based strategy planning approach can be tested by evaluating whether product superiority improves customer value. A survey of 4105 respondents from 626 B2B companies statistically measured how much value customers derived from product and service quality, as measured by their overall satisfaction. The study showed the strategy area provided 19% of customer value. The remaining value was created by satisfying customer needs via communication, safety, and billing and pricing.

The results are not isolated. Between 2013 and 2018, several companies provided similar data on customer value drivers. The firms were from different sectors: industrial distribution, aeronautics testing equipment, engineering and construction, oilfield services, computer software, and chemicals manufacturing. What percentage of overall customer value was attributed to strategy areas related to product quality? As shown in Table 6.1, quality accounted for zero customer value in some cases.

For each company, senior executives also estimated how much product quality contributed to overall customer value. Their answers ranged between 70% and 80%. When asked why, the executives provided answers such as, "We know this to be the case. After all, it's what our entire strategy is based upon," "We have invested in R&D to differentiate ourselves, and customers see it," "Customers want the innovative products and services," and "Product differentiation is critical to lead the market." The results showed a clear disconnect between the focus of budget-based strategy plans, R&D, innovation, customer needs, and overall customer value. The executives reinforced the results detailed in Chap. 5, which indicated R&D investments, a

Table 6.1 Importance of product/service in driving customer value

Industry	Company size	Quality measure	Percentage of value proposition attributed to quality
Industrial distribution	$1–2 billion	Product quality	35%
Oilfield services	$1–2 billion	Product quality	29%
Industrial pipeline	$1–2 billion	Innovation/R&D	0%
Testing equipment—aerospace	$10–50 million	Product quality	0%
Engineering and projects	$5–8 billion	Product quality	17%
Engineering and projects cohort	$50 billion (five firms)	Product quality	12%
Software	Over $400 billion	Product quality	11%
Banking	$40 billion	Competitive rates/fees	12%
Integrated facilities management	$2–3 billion	Quality of on-site products and services	27%
Healthcare software	$20 million	Quality of software product	31%
B2B companies	$5 million–$400 billion	Product/service quality	19%

precondition for superior products and services, were not predictive of financial performance.

Was product differentiation, a cornerstone of many strategy plans, related to financial performance? An examination of B2B companies' mission statements showed a strong belief in product and service quality as a key strategy objective. Sixty-two percent of the statements emphasized differentiation through quality. The survey of executive MBA students reported in Chap. 3 asked respondents to rank, by importance, the eight strategy areas for driving sales and financial performance. Among them, product and service quality consistently ranked as a top factor. When respondents were asked about the rankings, they said:

- "We need to have better products with more features to increase pricing power."
- "We need to invest in product development to differentiate our brand from competition."
- "Without superior products and services, we cannot be market leaders."

Table 6.2 Financial performance and perceived product quality

Financial outcomes	Product quality		Are financial outcomes different based on product quality?
	Below average/ average	Above average	
Sales (billions)	$13.5 billion	$13.33 billion	No
Gross margin (billions)	$4.7 billion	$4.6 billion	No

To test the notion, the database of 4105 survey respondents was divided into two groups: companies rated as above average on perceived product quality and those rated average/below average on perceived product quality. After statistically removing the effect of company size, industry type, and other characteristics, the analysis compared the groups' sales and gross margins. As shown in Table 6.2, the average sales for the firms rated at or below average on product quality was $13.5 billion. Average sales for the firms rated above average on product quality was $13.33 billion. No statistical difference emerged between the groups. Results for gross margins were similar. The average gross margin for the firms rated at or below average on product quality, $4.7 billion, was statistically similar to the average gross margin for firms rated above average on product quality, $4.6 billion.

A central tenet of budget-based planning is its emphasis on efficiency through cost cutting and expense reduction. To what extent does emphasizing efficiency in strategy planning affect financial outcomes? Previous studies have shown mixed results. A 2002 landmark study directly compared the financial benefits of emphasizing revenue expansion through increased customer satisfaction and/or cost reductions to the benefits of quality improvements, such as standardization, six sigma, and reduced defect rates.[18] The study surveyed 186 managers at 70 business units in different companies to measure beliefs about the firms' emphasis on cost reduction or revenue expansion. The researchers then related the measures to ROA and stock returns. The results showed a revenue emphasis had a statistically positive effect on financial outcomes, while a cost emphasis had no effect. The authors concluded, "The cost emphasis had no effect on primary or secondary measures of performance. The two faces of quality (revenue expansion through customer satisfaction and cost reduction through efficiency) are not two sides of the same coin...our research indicates that a revenue emphasis may be the most effective." The study showed managers' beliefs about achieving cost reductions and efficiency goals did not translate into financial benefits. A budget-based strategy planning approach was less likely to benefit the bottom-line than a planning process linked to customer needs.

A 2005 study used a sample of 77 firms with data from 1994 to 2000.[19] Instead of measuring managers' beliefs about satisfaction and efficiency, the study measured customer satisfaction and efficiency levels. In other words, it did not focus on the strategy planning process, but rather measured the outcomes of increased customer satisfaction and resulting cost efficiencies. Then, it related both outcomes to long-term company value. The results showed achieving cost efficiency increased long-term value negligibly if a firm was unable to increase customer satisfaction. However, when firms increased cost efficiency along with customer satisfaction, the increase in long-term value was dramatic. The authors concluded, "For a typical firm in our database with a market value of $46 billion, a one-point increase in customer satisfaction is worth $1.613 billion in market value to a high efficiency firm, while a one point increase in [customer satisfaction] for a low efficiency firm adds $298 million in market value." In other words, the benefit of efficiency was 5.4 times more when a company also satisfied its customers' needs. Clearly, firms focusing their strategy planning on efficiency left a lot of money on the table: $1.315 billion on average.

The issue can also be explored using the dataset of 4105 customer surveys from 626 B2B companies collected from 2017 to 2018. Firm efficiency was calculated using data envelopment analysis (DEA), a technique developed in the operations research literature and often used to study company strategy.[20] DEA computes efficiency by comparing a company's ratio of outputs and inputs to its peers. The most efficient firms use few inputs or produce large quantities of outputs. To assess the efficiency focus of each firm in the sample, the model used overall customer satisfaction as the output variable and customer satisfaction in the eight strategy areas as the inputs. The most efficient firms either needed the fewest strategy areas to produce the same overall customer satisfaction or created higher overall customer satisfaction with the same strategy area inputs. The results confirmed the findings of the 2005 study. The average gross margins for four groups (i.e., low customer satisfaction/low efficiency, low customer satisfaction/high efficiency, high customer satisfaction/low efficiency, high customer satisfaction/high efficiency) are displayed in Fig. 6.1 and summarized as follows:

- Firms with low customer satisfaction and low efficiency had low gross margins ($3.3 billion).
- Firms with high efficiency and low customer satisfaction had the lowest gross margins ($2.9 billion), even lower than firms with low customer satisfaction and low efficiency. The high efficiency and low customer satisfaction condition was considered a sign of an internally focused company.

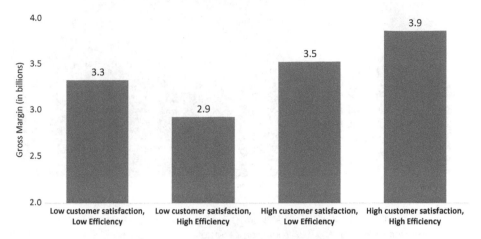

Fig. 6.1   Customer satisfaction, efficiency, and gross margin

- Firms with high customer satisfaction and low efficiency achieved significant gross margin improvements ($3.5 billion). Achieving high customer satisfaction at the cost of efficiency was considered a sign of a customer-focused company.
- Firms with high customer satisfaction and high efficiency achieved the top gross margins ($3.9 billion).

Achieving the highest level of financial performance required increasing customer focus along with operational excellence. Attempting to achieve operational excellence or efficiency without a customer focus yielded the worst performance.

Do any specific strategy areas consistently drive financial performance? The three firms in the B2B benchmark with the highest market value in their industries were Apple, Johnson & Johnson, and ExxonMobil. The three firms with the smallest market value were 1PM Industries, Ambient Water Corporation, and Arista Financial Corporation. Were the two groups systematically different in terms of customers' satisfaction with one or another strategy area? Figure 6.2 shows that the customer satisfaction index of six firms across the eight areas was comparable. The index ranges from 0 to 100, with higher scores implying higher customer satisfaction:

- Apple (85), Arista Financial (79), and Johnson & Johnson (79) had higher scores on ongoing service and support than 1PM Industries (74).
- ExxonMobil (79) and Johnson & Johnson (78) had higher scores on pricing and billing than Apple (77) and Arista Financial (64).
- Arista Financial (86) and ExxonMobil (83) had higher scores on product and service quality than Johnson & Johnson (81) and 1PM Industries (79).

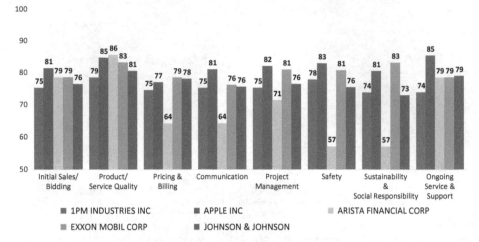

Fig. 6.2 Comparison of relative satisfaction with strategic areas

No obvious magic formula emerged for selecting the most important strategy areas. Research across dozens of companies and more than 600 companies in the study dataset showed the strategy areas driving overall customer value differ from industry to industry and company to company. They must be statistically determined for each company individually.

6.3   Conclusion

The budget-based strategy planning approach is popular with senior executives because it provides a clear sense of real and perceived control over resources. By increasing or decreasing the budget allocated to a specific initiative, executives can clearly signal their priorities to internal and external stakeholders. The process also provides executives with a credible way to test their hypotheses about what drives financial value.

Yet there are disadvantages to the approach. To a large extent, it is inconsistent with some of the fundamental beliefs senior executives bring to strategy planning. When executives allocate budget to a specific initiative, they are expressing a belief that it improves performance. For example, many executives believe product superiority improves customer value, financial performance is based on product differentiation, and increased efficiency is the key to success. Budgetary decisions, such as prioritizing R&D and innovation and improving efficiency through cost reduction, are entrenched beliefs. Yet, as the analysis shows, the beliefs are not supported by large-scale databases. Efficient firms do not necessarily have higher margins, and customers do not value products as much as many executives believe.

Notes

1. Ackoff, Russell (1970), "A concept of corporate planning," *Long Range Planning*, 3(1), 2–8.
2. Ackoff, Russell (1981), "On the use of models in corporate planning," *Strategic Management Journal*, 2(4), 353–359.
3. Langley, Ann (1988), "The roles of formal strategic planning," *Long Range Planning*, 21(3), 40–50.
4. Feldman, Martha S., and James G. March (1981), "Information in organizations as signal and symbol," *Administrative Science Quarterly*, June (1), 171–186.
5. Naylor, Thomas H., and Horst Schauland (1976), "A survey of users of corporate planning models," *Management Science*, 22(9), 927–937.
6. CFO Innovation Staff (2015), "Survey: Strategic planning, people management most crucial for CFO success," *CFO Innovation Asia*, May 12, 3.
7. Dye, Renee, and Olivier Sibony (2007), "How to improve strategic planning," *McKinsey Quarterly*, August 1, 40–48.
8. Woo, Carolyn (1983), "Evaluation of the strategies and performance of low ROI market share leaders," *Strategic Management Journal*, 4(2), 123–135.
9. Woo, Carolyn (1983), "Evaluation of the strategies and performance of low ROI market share leaders," *Strategic Management Journal*, 4(2), 123–135.
10. Capon, Noel, John U. Farley, and James M. Hulbert (1994), "Strategic planning and financial performance: more evidence," *Journal of Management Studies*, 31(1), 105–110.
11. Capon, Noel, John U. Farley, and James M. Hulbert (1994), "Strategic planning and financial performance: more evidence," *Journal of Management Studies*, 31(1), 105–110.
12. Capon, Noel, John U. Farley, and James M. Hulbert (1994), "Strategic planning and financial performance: more evidence," *Journal of Management Studies*, 31(1), 105–110.
13. Corkery, Michael (2016), "Wells Fargo fined $185 million for fraudulently opening accounts," *The New York Times*, September 8.
14. Egan, Matt (2017), "Wells Fargo dumps toxic 'cross selling' metric," *CNN*, January 13.
15. Reuters Staff (2020), "Buffet's Berkshire slashes Wells Fargo stake," *Reuters*, September 4.
16. Gryta, Thomas, and Ted Mann (2018), "GE powered the American century—Then it burned out," *The Wall Street Journal*, December 14.
17. Mittal, Vikas, Eugene W. Anderson, Akin Sayrak, and Pandu Tadikamalla (2005), "Dual emphasis and the long-term financial impact of customer satisfaction," *Marketing Science*, 24(4), 544–555.
18. Rust, Roland T., Christine Moorman, and Peter R. Dickson (2002), "Getting return on quality: Revenue expansion, cost reduction, or both?" *Journal of Marketing*, 66(October), 7–24.

19. Mittal, Vikas, Eugene W. Anderson, Akin Sayrak, and Pandu Tadikamalla (2005), "Dual emphasis and the long-term financial impact of customer satisfaction," *Marketing Science*, 24(4), 544–555.
20. Mittal, Vikas, Eugene W. Anderson, Akin Sayrak, and Pandu Tadikamalla (2005), "Dual emphasis and the long-term financial impact of customer satisfaction," *Marketing Science*, 24(4), 544–555.

7

Strategy Planning Inhibitors

Strategy planning absorbs time, attention, and resources from all management levels. But it is hard to deny the importance of the process, as it is intended to help with goal setting, resource allocation, implementation plans, and accountability.

Surveyed CEOs consistently say they value strategy planning, and senior executives and managers say the process is essential. However, the executives tend to overestimate strategy planning's financial benefits. A detailed review of three predominant strategy planning approaches in Chaps. 4, 5, and 6 provides a deep understanding of their potential pitfalls and why the process fails to deliver the financial results CEOs and other senior executives expect.

Further discussions with CEOs and observations about strategy planning in large and small companies in a variety of industries reveal several inhibitors to the process. A strategy inhibitor can be an executive's behavioral tendency or biases downplaying the need to collect and use comprehensive information. Inevitably, strategy planning processes riddled with inhibitors lead to flawed plans and doomed execution. Worse, the inhibitors prevent executives from evolving as leaders, thwarting their CEOs' expectations. Understanding inhibitors is therefore crucial for CEOs to ensure their strategy process is robust, their senior executives maximize their contribution to the process, and their strategy is linked to financial success.

In discussions with company executives, seven strategy planning inhibitors emerge as the most common roadblocks to the process.

© The Author(s), under exclusive license to Springer Nature Switzerland AG 2021
V. Mittal, S. Sridhar, *Focus*, https://doi.org/10.1007/978-3-030-70720-0_7

7.1   Inhibitor 1: Confusing Salience with Importance

Salience is the extent to which some factors and perceptual elements become prominent in a person's decision-making, despite other factors being more consequential for desired outcomes. In terms of decision-making, factors become salient when they are top-of-mind and are easy to recall, remember, imagine, and elaborate upon. Unfortunately, being salient in a person's mind does not mean a factor has any impact on outcomes of interest. Instead, the importance of a decision factor is based on the extent to which it is statistically associated with a desired outcome.

The more strongly an input or decision factor is quantitatively associated with an outcome of interest, the more important it should be to the decision maker. Unfortunately, important business decision factors are not always salient to executives. Conversely, many salient decision factors can turn out to be unimportant for outcomes of interest.

Why do executives ignore importance and use salience in decision-making? Salience is based on ease and probability of recall and repetition, while importance must be determined through formal statistical analysis. Many executives therefore use salient information in the strategy planning process for its convenience. They do not take the time to determine if the information is truly important for their desired outcomes.

In Chap. 2, CEOs describe many strategy planning exercises in which executives rely on salience and ignore the importance of strategy factors. When one company's HR group stressed its training programs and the product development group created new offerings—both intending to contribute to sales growth—their senior executives had set strategy based on salience and ignored the relative importance of each program. When the senior executives at another firm adopted integrity, safety, and innovation as their core values, they were relying on salience and ignoring strategy area importance.

A 1979 study demonstrated the biasing effect of salience in everyday life. The study surveyed people about their estimated risk of dying from various causes, such as drowning, car accidents, murder, heart attacks, and cancer.[1] The authors found participants' risk estimates were higher for causes mentioned more often in local news than others. In other words, salience due to local-news coverage biased people's risk estimates for an outcome, dying. Another study found people judged the frequency of lethal events based on disproportionate exposure, memorability, or imaginability, all factors enhancing salience.[2]

In a study of business students and executives, researchers experimentally manipulated the salience of various decision factors. They found the factors' salience affected decision outcomes among the participants.[3] Executives were no less immune to the ill-effects of salience than novice students were. Another study showed executives relied on information salience at all stages of strategy decision-making because it was perceived as simplifying the process.[4] The executives focused on salient strategy areas while ignoring important priorities, especially when setting goals to achieve desirable outcomes.

The ill-effects of relying on salience and ignoring importance were particularly evident at FOODCO, the lunch-focused restaurant chain discussed in Chap. 1. A sharp disconnect emerged between the salience of strategy areas for FOODCO's owner and that of the areas important to customers (see Fig. 7.1). The strategy areas of "high-quality food" and "expanded menu" were salient to the owner, as reflected in their high recall probability. In contrast, a short waiting time, simple menu, and parking were important for FOODCO's customers but not salient to the owner. The importance of each area can be seen in Panel B of Fig. 7.1. The statistical link between a short waiting time and customer value was high. A simple menu and parking were also critical. An expanded menu was low in importance due to its minimal association with the outcome of interest—customer value. Relying only on salience, the owner unintentionally created a poorly aligned strategy plan.

To counteract the damaging effects of salience and prioritize strategy areas based on importance, executives must first conduct a rigorous analysis. They must clearly define their desired outcome and a set of critical inputs. The inputs' importance must be calculated based on how strongly each is linked to

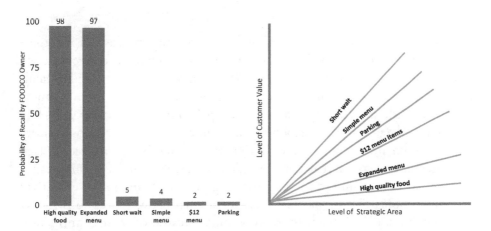

Fig. 7.1 Strategic area salience and importance for FOODCO

the desired outcome. The process involves linking performance in different strategy areas to the outcome while statistically controlling for confounding extraneous factors.

To calculate the importance of a strategy factor without mental biases, senior executives at a firm must implement the following steps:

1. *Identify the unit of interest.* The unit may be customers, employees, geographic regions, product lines, territories, or business divisions.
2. *Develop a measurable metric for the relevant strategy outcome.* The appropriate strategy outcome is usually customer value, as measured through surveys, or a financial metric, such as revenue, quantity sold, sales, margin, or ROI.
3. *Develop a performance metric for the strategy areas evaluated.* The metric can be based on actual data (e.g., operational metrics), perceptions from customer or employee surveys, or secondary research (e.g., industry association ratings). Survey-based performance metrics provide useful insights only if the survey is carefully designed.
4. *Use rigorous statistical analysis to isolate the magnitude of association between each strategy area and the relevant strategy outcome.* For most companies, the process involves engaging analytics experts. Going beyond simple correlations, the goal is to isolate the unique association between a strategy area and the outcome after controlling for confounding factors. Relative importance can be calculated as the percentage change in the desired outcome as a result of a unit shift in an input.
5. *Depict the relative importance of inputs.* The percentage change in the desired outcome as a result of a unit shift in an input can be used to prioritize strategy areas.

What impedes senior executives' ability to use importance and renounce salience? First, executives fail to isolate and precisely define the correct strategy outcomes. Outcomes like "shareholder value" may be too vague and difficult to measure to create the input-output analysis necessary to calculate importance. Second, the strategy planning group in many companies lacks the resources—data, statistical expertise, and time—to measure and quantify strategy input importance. Third and most importantly, firms typically lack the discipline, rigor, and patience needed to calculate and use importance rather than salience in the strategy planning process. Many senior executives are comfortable using salience, which relies on their biased perceptions, is easy to ascertain, and is difficult to prove wrong. Because of their confirmation bias—the tendency to confirm preexisting beliefs—few executives undertake rigorous data collection and analysis to determine the importance of strategy areas to align strategy implementation.[5]

Two complementary studies provide an example where nursing home executives broke the curse of salience and used importance to set strategy priorities.[6] The nursing homes wanted to decrease employee turnover, a persistent and chronic problem. The researchers asked 47 employees to state their reasons for keeping or leaving their nursing home jobs. Higher pay and better benefits emerged as salient reasons, along with perceived lack of respect, management's poor attitude, and a desire to engage in patient advocacy. The reasons were top-of-mind for participants and therefore salient. Rather than assume salience equated with importance, the researchers statistically computed importance. They surveyed 620 employees (the unit of interest) and asked them to rate their satisfaction with different inputs (i.e., strategy areas, such as pay, health insurance, and supervisor respect). They then statistically related the inputs to actual employee turnover, the strategy outcome. The analysis eliminated extraneous factors like employee age and nursing home location. The two factors most associated with employee turnover were receiving health insurance (41% importance weight) and promotion opportunities (39% importance weight). Hourly pay, with an importance weight of 0%, had no association with turnover. By increasing access to healthcare coverage and creating career and promotion pathways, the executives decreased turnover. Had they continued relying on salience, they would have likely focused on increasing pay and supervisory respect and improving management attitudes while ignoring the two most important factors impacting employee turnover.

7.2   Inhibitor 2: Intuitive Leaps

Intuition is defined as "a judgment or choice made through a subconscious synthesis of information drawn from diverse experiences."[7] An intuitive leap involves "recognition of a familiar situation and the straightforward but partially subconscious application of previous learning related to that situation."[8] In strategy decisions, intuitive leaps occur when executives use previously held notions, assumptions, and beliefs to draw cause-and-effect conclusions about different and disparate situations. An executive taking an intuitive leap applies a simple cause-and-effect model to a complex reality and ignores intermediate factors linking inputs and outputs. The nursing home executives made an intuitive leap when drawing conclusions based on conversations with a few dozen employees. They assumed higher pay would decrease turnover. The leap was based on a belief not backed by any empirical reality in the executives' organizational context.

When making intuitive leaps, executives fail to assign relative importance weights to cause-and-effect relationships and assume causal relationships are absolute. Panel A of Fig. 7.2 shows the intuitive leap the nursing home executives would have made by assuming that higher pay was the sole determinant of reduced employee turnover. They could not determine whether the importance weight of higher pay was, for example, 10% or 40%. And they would have ignored other factors driving the outcome.

Panel B of Fig. 7.2 shows the point at which the nursing home executives stopped relying on intuitive leaps. First, they understood employee turnover was not related to a single factor but multiple factors operating through turnover intention. Second, they realized they could prioritize multiple input factors based on their importance. The process helped them stop using an all-or-nothing approach to strategy.

During the strategy planning process, intuitive leaps often manifest as bold, plausible, and inspirational statements. However, they are in fact oversimplified versions of reality and ignore underlying complexity. As described by the CEOs in Chap. 2, functional executives often rely on consulting reports that

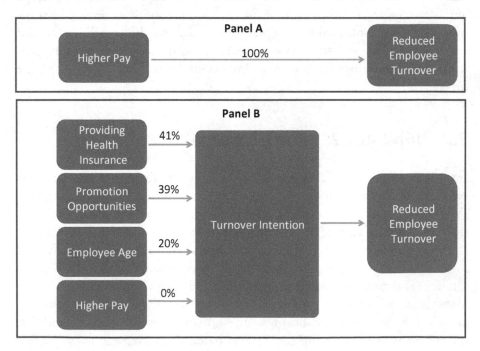

Fig. 7.2 Intuitive leaps at nursing homes

provide simple solutions for complex problems. Industry reports making statements like, "employee engagement leads to higher productivity" or "R&D is related to company profitability," often foster intuitive leaps. As executives make leaps about their functional strategy priorities, they are unable to focus and sequence the priorities, a key concern outlined by the CEOs interviewed.

Intuitive leaps are easily recognized. They are presented as plausible-sounding causal statements but ignore the causality and strength of the relationship considered. In Chap. 2, examples abound. A firm's senior vice presidents of HR and operations who claimed more than 30 safety indicators improved employee engagement, margins, and productivity made an intuitive leap. The company had not undertaken any analysis to determine the relative importance weight of the different metrics, nor had it decided its desired strategy outcome. The marketing director who claimed sales growth occurred due to a better product lineup also made an intuitive leap. The CEOs interviewed in Chap. 2 correctly identified the errors often occurred because the executives involved in strategy planning could not even agree on the appropriate strategy inputs and outputs. Computing their importance weights was far from the executives' minds.

The intuitive leap by FOODCO's owner is shown in Panel A of Fig. 7.3. The owner assumed a single factor, an expanded menu, increased sales. However, many strategy inputs affected sales through their impact on customer value. Unless strategy areas' relative importance weights are determined through careful analysis using statistically valid datasets, executives are bound to mislead the strategy planning process.

Intuitive leaps establish false associations and exaggerate reality. The FOODCO owner's intuitive leap led the strategy process astray in two respects. First, it conflated the salience of expanded menu choice with its importance. Second, it established a false association, suggesting with 100% certainty that high-quality offerings would increase sales.

Several factors contributed to the FOODCO owner's intuitive leap. The owner used heuristics to speed up and simplify decision-making.[9] Heuristics rely on simple cause-and-effect assumptions. They work for simple, everyday decisions like, "if I take a shorter route, I will get to work sooner." They do not work for complex strategy. FOODCO's owner also projected salient information into a complex situation. The owner recalled examples of employees and customers at high sales locations appreciating a wide selection of offerings. The top-of-mind instances led the owner to draw the incorrect conclusion that quality offerings impacted sales. The owner missed the reality that locations with low sales offered the same menu items.

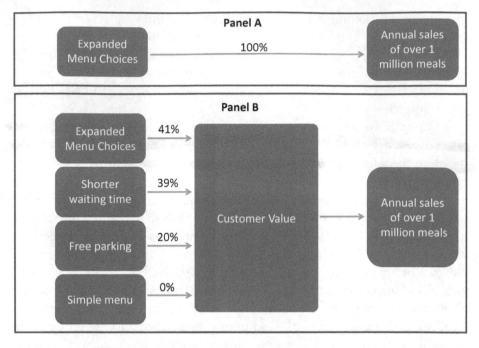

Fig. 7.3 Intuitive leaps at FOODCO

The executive vice president of sales at a large energy construction company emphasized safety as the firm's strategy crux. "We cannot even qualify to bid on a project without a perfect safety record," the executive said. "Clearly, without safety, there can be no strategy, since the company will shut down. Things like project management, ongoing service and support, communications—I've never had a customer mention them." The conclusion was contrary to statistical evidence showing many of the firm's competitors had lower safety scores but higher customer satisfaction ratings and margins. Furthermore, evidence showed many safety incidents resulted from communication breakdowns, inadequate project management, and lack of ongoing service and support. Rather than consider the underlying causal model based on evidence, the executive continued to believe safety investments should drive the company's strategy.

Intuitive leaps ignore multiple determinants of a strategy outcome. At FOODCO, a statistical analysis showed sales were most associated with (1) the menu having fewer items than average, (2) availability of free and ample parking, and (3) short wait times when ordering. FOODCO's sales had no association with a large menu or item quality. The owner made an intuitive leap and overrepresented the effect of menu offerings while ignoring the factors most associated with sales.

Through confirmation bias, executives show their preference for information supporting preexisting attitudes while ignoring information opposing them.[10] When FOODCO's owner learned competitors with simplified menus and reduced wait times had increased sales, he said: "Agree, but they have a different strategy than ours. I've personally had customers come and tell me how much they appreciate the offerings on our menu." Similarly, the construction company vice president of sales refused to acknowledge that competitors with lower safety scores were more successful in generating sales and margins.

Intuitive leaps ignore intervening processes. By directly linking menu offerings to sales, the FOODCO owner ignored intervening processes that generate the sales, or what statisticians call mediating processes.[11] Mediation occurs when the impact of a causal factor (e.g., menu offerings) on an outcome (e.g., sales) is transmitted through an intervening factor (e.g., customer value). Executives making intuitive leaps link variables directly and ignore the intermediate processes. Consider a person with a fever. Before deciding what medicine to prescribe, the physician must determine the factor causing the fever, a bacterial infection or virus. The doctor then prescribes a unique treatment depending on the mediating factor—the type of infection.

As shown in Panel B of Fig. 7.3, FOODCO's owner missed the mediating role of customer value in driving restaurant sales. The owner therefore failed to understand that factors beyond menu offerings delivered value and drove sales. Addressing a mediating factor, rather than a final outcome, allows for a precise and effective action plan. Addressing a fever by attacking the correct mediator—viral or bacterial infection—yields a more effective outcome for a patient than addressing only the final outcome of fever reduction.

How does strategy planning become riddled with intuitive leaps? In some cases, senior executives assume a strong, direct link between the company values espoused in their mission statements and outcomes like sales growth, even in the absence of statistically reliable evidence. Recall that 63% of CEOs believe having a mission statement enables better leadership and 53% believe it improves staff morale.[12] However, a study found no relationship between 25 mission statement components and average percentage change in sales and profits.[13]

In other cases, executives assume whatever worked at their previous job or company will work in their current job or company. The CEOs interviewed in Chap. 2 identified many situations where executives made intuitive leaps rooted in their own functional background. Finance believed cost cutting would increase company value. Marketing believed better branding and social media operations would optimize strategy. And manufacturing believed in lean production initiatives. In each case, the executives made intuitive leaps to justify and defend their favored initiatives.

FOODCO's CEO defended a large advertising budget because the organization's owner believed food quality and an expansive menu drove sales. But the evidence showed no provable link between food quality and sales or an expanded menu and sales. Furthermore, the chain's advertising spending did not correlate to sales. FOODCO operated like a patient taking aspirin to relieve a migraine without evidence aspirin relieves migraines. Worse, when confronted with the lack of evidence, the patient cited the one instance aspirin cured his migraine as evidence for taking a larger dose.

7.3   Inhibitor 3: Belief in Mythical Numbers

Max Singer pioneered the concept of mythical numbers in 1971 by asking a simple question: How much property is stolen by drug addicts in New York City on a yearly basis?[14] At the time, officials believed addicts stole between $2 billion and $5 billion worth of property and committed about half the city's crimes. The estimate was widely used by institutions like RAND Corporation, political figures like Howard Samuels, and the U.S. Attorney General to justify giving drug addiction priority attention. With a few simple calculations, Singer showed "that whereas it is widely assumed that addicts steal from $2 billion-$5 billion a year in New York City, the actual number is 10 times smaller, and that this can be demonstrated by five minutes of thought." Singer calculated that for addicts to steal $2 billion-$5 billion of property, they would have had to steal 20% of all durable and nondurable goods. The property theft estimate at the time was about 2%.

Singer's goal in the exercise was to examine people's attitudes toward numbers. He suggested very large numbers can acquire mythical stature, especially when related to ideas supporting preconceived notions. Over time, the mythical numbers are accepted as a given—an unfalsifiable predicate, an unassailable fact. They are then used to justify actions and initiatives without thinking about their plausibility. With such a large amount of property loss in New York City, who could argue against an initiative to spend $20 million to fight drug addiction?

Most mythical numbers originate from consulting studies and are intended to establish broad and eye-popping trends or provide a snapshot of an entire industry, a country's economy, or the global economy. The numbers are extremely large, and senior executives extrapolate them to their own company and present action plans based on them. Because executives find it difficult to grasp their magnitude, the mythical numbers gain a vitality of their own.

Mythical numbers disrupt the strategy planning process for many firms. Based on the statement, "[digitalization] can assist in providing electricity to the 1.1 billion people who still lack access to it,"[15] the chief information officer of a small oilfield services company sought to increase the company's digital footprint to gain market share.

"Every dollar invested in marketing advertising contributes to the bottom-line," said the chief marketing officer of a company with $500 million in sales. "An industry study[16] shows that companies on average spend 12% of their revenue on marketing." The marketing executive was seeking a budget increase from $5 million to $60 million. Executives tend to use mythical numbers as irrefutable evidence to support their priorities during strategy planning. Because they are difficult to refute, mythical numbers are used as evidence to continue supporting previously tentative assertions during strategy planning.[17] After all, who would argue with the importance of digitalization? And how could one show digitalization does not provide electricity access to more than 1 billion people?

Executives at SCHOOLCO, the school district described in Chap. 1, made a large number of investments in extracurricular activities. They justified them using statements relying on mythical numbers, such as: "I recently read a study showing that students who participate in sports and music are four times more successful than students who do not" or "Ten minutes of music a day can improve SAT scores by 15 points and the lifetime wages of an average American by $800,000, according to new research mentioned in a newspaper article I just read." While extracurricular activities might indeed be valuable, the executives used mythical numbers to justify investments while their schools failed to meet minimum academic standards for seven consecutive years. An objective analysis across all the district's schools showed no statistically reliable association between extracurricular activities and student academic achievement. In many instances, investments in extracurriculars came at the expense of academic services, such as tutoring in math and reading. Some principals of academically failing schools vehemently defended extracurricular activities while sidestepping academic discussions. They continued to argue the investments would make the students four times more successful.

A presentation for a small oilfield services company opened with the following mythical number and intuitive leap: "The oil and gas industry is seven times more likely to have a safety incident than all other leading industries—claiming well over a thousand lives each year." The presenter made the case the company needed to invest in safety "to win new business, because a company cannot be on the bidding list without an impeccable safety record." Safety data on oilfield services companies showed the sector was the safest in the industry, the presenter's company had a good safety record, and the firm had never been disqualified from bidding. Objective data did not support additional investments in safety. At another company, an executive team wanted to support the core value of employee engagement. The team charged an analyst to find facts supporting engagement's importance. After research, the analyst presented a mythical number—more than 80% of CEOs of successful companies believed employee engagement was an organizational imperative. Based on the mythical number and an intuitive leap that employee engagement leads to company success, the executive team decided to push ahead with engagement initiatives.

One way to counter mythical numbers is to engage in counterfactual thinking and argue against the reported fact. The exercise, as demonstrated by Singer's influential article, entails a logical approach, looking at numbers from all vantage points. For example, consider the mythical number in the statement, "Over 80% of CEOs of successful companies believe employee engagement is an organizational imperative." How were companies rated as being successful? What other imperatives besides employee engagement did the CEOs rate? Among the rated imperatives, how many rated higher or lower than 80%? How many CEOs were included in the study? What does it mean for something to be an organizational imperative? Are there successful organizations where employees are not as engaged? Amazon, one of the world's most successful companies, has been frequently cited for low employee engagement.[18] Another industry report has chided successful companies such as Amazon, eBay, Gilead Sciences, Monster Beverage, Walt Disney, and Wells Fargo for their response to the COVID-19 crisis and inequality issues.[19] Such counterfactuals can deflate the influence of mythical numbers on strategy planning.

7.4   Inhibitor 4: Staying Put

For most companies, the strategy planning process is part of a stream of activities intended to identify, budget, and plan for new initiatives, projects, and activities. Unfortunately, once resources are allocated to a project, executives find it difficult to reverse course, even when the project's prognosis turns negative. One group of researchers asked senior executives participating in a strategy simulation to allocate resources to different initiatives and projects.[20] Half of the executives received no background input, while the other half was presented details of the previous year's budget. The second group aligned its allocation closely to the previous allocation, despite it having little correlation with market conditions and potential for future return. In other words, executives stayed put. The tendency is referred to as the status quo bias, which also manifests as the sunk-cost effect.

Many executives continue to throw good money after bad,[21] exhibiting ongoing resource commitment to courses of action regardless of their likelihood of success.[22] The tendency has been documented in hundreds of studies summarized in a variety of systematic reviews and meta-analyses.[23] The results run counter to CEOs' desire to focus and sequence their strategy work, which includes setting budgets, initiatives, priorities, and activities. In many companies strategy planning becomes an excuse for senior executives to add initiatives and expand existing initiatives.

Senior executives have many reasons to stay put or escalate their commitment to a failing course of action. First, they find comfort in familiarity, defined as accumulated stimulus-related experiences. The more an executive is exposed to an initiative, the more familiar with it he or she becomes.[24] As familiarity grows, it becomes easier to perform a task and analyze information pertaining to it. Less mental effort is required to analyze the information. The executive's ability to remember information about the task improves, and mental models for the task become refined. The comfort propels executives to stay put in existing initiatives. A 2001 paper compared preferences for electricity providers among 1500 consumers falling into two groups: (1) high-reliability customers experiencing approximately three outages and (2) low-reliability customers experiencing approximately 15 outages.[25] Among the high-reliability group, 60.2% chose to stay with the current company rather than a 30% cheaper but unreliable option. Among the low-reliability group, 58.3% chose to stay with the current company rather than move to a 30% more expensive but reliable company. Executives are prone to similar behaviors. Time after time, even after realizing a strategy initiative is not meeting its promise, they maintain the status quo rather than change course.

Executives also feel loss aversion, the tendency to take bigger risks to avoid further losses.[26] Executives with an investment in an unsuccessful initiative are in a loss domain, making them motivated to take on risk. The risk taking manifests as further investment in the unsuccessful initiative, with the hope of turning it around.[27] As an example, long-shot bets at race tracks become more frequent toward the end of the day, when participants incurring losses in previous bets are likely to take higher risks.[28] A 1988 paper analyzed the selection of health plans among 9185 Harvard University employees and retirement funds among 850,000 members of the Teachers Insurance and Annuity Association. In both cases, evidence showed people remained committed to their original decisions "even though the transition costs may be small and the importance great."[29] Likewise, executives stick with underperforming strategy initiatives, making increasingly risky investments with the hope of turning things around. Indeed, strategy initiatives become more risk-seeking as a company's economic situation becomes more precarious, as measured by bankruptcy probability.[30]

Companies and their divisions fear resource dependence.[31] In an organizational ecosystem, executives and the functions or divisions they run are not autonomous but interdependent and replete with uncertainty. To reduce interdependence and uncertainty, executives often expand existing initiatives to acquire more resources for them.[32] In school districts, for example, initiative-dependent grants provide control over resources, increase executive power, and reduce uncertainty. Rather than determining if a grant is necessary, district administrators see renewing it as a key priority. Another example of staying put comes from Nobel Prize winner Milton Friedman, who cites a study by James Payne.[33] Payne examined 14 government hearings on budgeting issues. Among the 1060 witnesses testifying, 1014 favored spending, while only seven opposed it (145 to 1). Interestingly, 47% of the witnesses were federal administrators, 10% were state and local officials, and 6% were congresspeople, meaning 63% of the witnesses were government employees.[34]

Many executives use budget-based planning to maintain the status quo and stay put. They use the "percentage of last year" approach, making minimal changes to their annual budget and preserving most initiatives from the existing strategy plan. In other companies, mid-level executives select specific values and mission elements to justify their favorite initiatives. At FACILITYCO (see Chap. 1 for a full description), senior executives and frontline employees evaluated whether to "continue" or "discontinue" 27 initiatives. Only seven initiatives were elected to be continued by more than 50% of frontline employees and executives. Respondents were ambivalent about one initiative and said the firm should discontinue 19 initiatives. Yet, when executives from different functions (e.g., marketing, HR, sales, and finance) were asked to determine which of the 19 initiatives to eliminate, they could not agree on a single one.

The tendency to stay put in existing initiatives and projects can severely damage a firm's strategy planning. The practice directly increases costs without necessarily increasing revenues, a clear case of capital misallocation. Rather than putting capital to its best use, firms allocate it to low-productivity projects simply to continue them. The strategy also makes executives more vulnerable to the planning fallacy, where individuals are likely to underestimate the cost of initiatives and their completion time, while overestimating their benefits.[35] Studies of government projects have shown planners are also inaccurate when forecasting costs. In one study, the executives were off by 44.7% for rail projects, 33.8% for bridges and tunnels, and 20.4% for roads.[36]

Finally, staying put increases strategy complexity. The higher the number of existing initiatives, the higher the direct and indirect cost of coordination to ensure they are implemented with fidelity. But as initiative numbers increase linearly, overall costs increase exponentially. Consider again General Electric, an iconic company suffering stock price declines from 2008 to 2018. One reason for GE's losses was the complexity of its different divisions and business groups, along with their many strategy initiatives.[37] Complexity and increased coordination has been blamed for declining value among many diversified firms. A 1995 study found such firms lost on average 13%–15% in value,[38] a conclusion supported by a 1994 study showing diversified firms had lower value than pure-play companies.[39]

A 2007 study found the likelihood of successfully shutting down a project is highest when it is about 50% complete but lowest when it is either 10% or 90% complete.[40] At 10%, firms tended to give the projects time, where at 90% they simply wanted to complete the projects. The study authors recommended strategy projects should have an automatic sunset clause and be evaluated at 50% complete. For most companies, the survival of initiatives completing the initial launch phase is effectively assured, regardless of performance. Management consultant Peter Drucker advocates a process of systematic abandonment through a periodic, unsentimental project review. As Drucker wrote in 1985, "nothing so powerfully concentrates a man's mind on innovation as the knowledge that the present product or service will be abandoned in the foreseeable future."[41] Former ExxonMobil CEO Lee Raymond required his corporate-planning team to identify 3%–5% of the company's assets for potential disposal every year. ExxonMobil's divisions were allowed to retain assets placed in the group only if they could demonstrate a tangible and compelling turnaround program. The burden was on the business units to prove why assets should not be disposed of, rather than the other way around.[42]

Implementing an approach like ExxonMobil's requires senior executives to develop measurable criteria to assess strategy initiatives and projects at various stages. As shown in Chap. 2, CEOs believe strategy outcomes such as customer value and sales can be used to gauge the relative importance of initiatives. By calculating their relative importance, executives can apply a common and standardized yardstick to evaluate otherwise incomparable projects. A manufacturing equipment distributor ranked 65 company-wide initiatives by their potential increase in customer value. Ten initiatives provided 71% of the lift, and among them, five provided 61% of the increase. The distributor's senior executives focused their effort on the five initiatives, putting 14 others on hold and dropping 46 initiatives completely. The strategy not only saved $15 million but also provided greater strategy clarity and focus and expanded margins.[43]

7.5   Inhibitor 5: More-Is-Better Thinking

Not only does most strategy planning display inertia—a tendency for staying put—but it also tends to expand and add to a company's portfolio of existing initiatives. Rarely do executives reduce or focus their initiative portfolio. Instead, they suffer from more-is-better thinking.

At TOOLCO (see Chap. 1 for a full description), executives objectively scored 90% of existing initiatives ineffective. But they decided to add two new initiatives and request a 29% budget increase rather than drop ineffective projects. An engineering construction company determined its win rate on bids was a paltry 32%. Rather than reviewing the low win rate and focusing attention on projects the firm was most likely to win, sales executives added to the salesforce and doubled the number of bids submitted to achieve the year's sales target.

One reason executives expand initiatives is their tendency to seek variety. For example, individuals choosing among fitness clubs have been shown to prefer a large variety of services.[44] Variety seeking happens for three reasons: (1) a desire for stimulation, (2) changes in the external environment, and (3) hedging against uncertainty. Much as individuals seek to diversify their stock portfolios, such as through index funds reflecting the broader market, executives often seek variety as a hedge against uncertainty. Many senior executives believe their companies' geographic markets, product offerings, market reach, and project portfolios should be diversified. But the tendency can run counter to CEOs' desire to achieve strategy focus.

Executives' perceived self-efficacy and the resulting positivity/optimism bias drives them to expand their project portfolio. Self-efficacy is a person's belief he or she has the necessary skills and ability to resolve an issue.[45] A study of decision makers in 2002 showed those with high self-efficacy were likely to allocate significant money and time to projects, downplaying the risks and accentuating the upside.[46] During strategy planning, executives frame most projects positively to attract resource allocation. A role-play study of managers showed they were optimistic about problem-solving initiatives even as they hurt overall firm performance.[47] During strategy planning, executives have a tendency to undertake new projects, despite having too many active projects.

Highly diversified portfolios of strategy initiatives, business units, or plants can add direct and indirect coordination costs and reduce ultimate returns.[48] While the direct costs of any initiative can be factored into its return, firms often fail to account fully for coordination costs. Ultimately, the indirect costs extract a diversification discount, meaning the total value of the portfolio may be lower than the sum of its parts.

At the individual level, research shows larger and expanded choice sets are detrimental, inducing information overload and raising the cognitive costs of comparing and evaluating options. The prospect of choosing from an extensive menu and making difficult trade-offs can bring about negative emotions.[49] A study of 899,631 employees enrolled in 647 retirement plans in 69 industries showed plans offering more investment funds were less likely to be selected. Plans with two funds drew a 75% participation rate, while plans with 59 funds earned a 60% rate.[50] As the number of funds available increased, participants made more conservative choices, investing less in equity funds. For every ten additional funds, the likelihood of avoiding equities increased by 2.87%.[51] Similarly, adding high-quality projects and initiatives to an executive's agenda makes decisions difficult, induces negative stress, and decreases outcome quality.

At one B2B manufacturing company, senior executives required a short pitch deck and cost-benefit analysis for any strategy initiative costing more than $500,000. The goal was to enforce discipline and discourage initiative proliferation. But managers made achieving the goal difficult. "I just know that I need enough of the buzzwords that my COO cares about in my presentation, justify it based on some industry trends or numbers, and show how it might be linked to one of the vision or value points," one manager said. "I should be able to get budgetary approval." The manager admitted to using salience, intuitive leaps, and mythical numbers to pass initiatives.

7.6   Inhibitor 6: Inwardly Focused and Discordant

Surveyed CEOs repeatedly say the strategy planning process tends to be internally focused and lacks a customer lens. Executives become focused on their own department or group, despite their best efforts. CEOs interested in a customer lens realize customers are the single-largest source of cash flow for any company, and cash flow drives shareholder satisfaction.[52] Over time, a company that can satisfy its customers' needs while improving cash flow can also meet its shareholders' objectives. The path from strategy planning to shareholder wealth maximization weaves through customer satisfaction. A strategy plan focused on creating shareholder wealth without incorporating customer satisfaction makes the company inwardly focused.

Take the example of Wells Fargo, where the company began focusing on opening new accounts and meeting internal sales targets. The firm gave no regard to customer satisfaction. Executives whose bonuses were tied to sales and new accounts became focused on inward-looking metrics, rather than satisfying customers' needs.[53] Even as the number of new accounts ballooned, customer dissatisfaction caught up with Wells Fargo, which eventually fired 5300 employees and was fined $185 million.[54]

SCHOOLCO and TOOLCO are two examples where executives internally focused the strategy planning process. The organizations justified many strategy planning initiatives based on goals like increasing sales or adding shareholder value. But they used inadequate metrics to monitor progress. The metrics served only internal stakeholders' needs. Over time, senior executives and middle managers become inwardly focused.

Executives at engineering and products firm EPCO (see Chap. 1 for a full description) measured more than 300 metrics for each project worth more than $40 million. The justification was to monitor profitability and ensure customer needs were met. Yet, an analysis of the metrics showed: (1) none of them captured customer ratings or opinions about project performance, (2) they captured only activity-based costs, and (3) the company could not match costs and billing to calculate realized profits during a project's life cycle. Because none of the metrics or activities related to customer value, the sponsoring executives justified them using salience and intuitive leaps. The result was a CEO's worst nightmare—deciding the strategy agenda through personal preferences of senior executives. In turn, the biased decision-making process impedes the CEO's ability to drive alignment throughout the organization, both laterally among senior executives and vertically among executives, middle managers, and frontline employees.

Companies often become inwardly focused for an illusion of control, defined as a higher expectation of success than is objectively warranted.[55] For example, when subjects in one study were able to choose a lottery ticket instead of being given the ticket, they estimated a higher chance of winning. In another study, participants asked to think deliberately about planning a personal goal showed more control over a subsequent unrelated task than a control group. Merely asking people to think about planning fostered an illusion of control.[56] The illusion of control gives individuals confidence, and studies have shown managers with a higher sense of self-efficacy are more willing to take risks and allocate resources to initiatives because they focus on upside.[57]

Internally focused projects foster an illusion of control and optimism among executives, who then create budgets, develop plans, and track metrics. Studies have shown that companies where executives have a high illusion of control make positively biased forecasts.[58] Combined with the tendency to continue existing projects and add more, the illusion of control fosters a favorable attitude toward internally focused initiatives. If the projects are based on executives' intuitive leaps, they can also lead to disagreement and interpersonal conflict, increasing the opportunities for misalignment.[59]

A genuine sense of strategy consensus is a critical imperative for success. A 1999 study examined companies across a range of sectors, including food products, tobacco, electronics, and electrical machinery.[60] The researchers obtained 101 surveys from marketing and R&D managers and measured strategy consensus and firm performance. The study measured strategy consensus via differences between marketing and R&D managers' responses to survey items about cost-leadership and differentiation strategies. Performance measures included effectiveness (the degree to which organizational goals were reached), efficiency (the relationship between organizational outputs and the inputs required), and adaptiveness (the ability to adapt to changes in environment). The researchers found consensus between marketing and R&D managers was correlated with all three performance measures. The findings were later corroborated by a meta-analysis of 21 studies linking strategy consensus and firm performance.[61] The studies in the meta-analysis surveyed executives and middle managers and captured subjective and objective measures of strategy consensus. The analysis found a positive relationship between consensus and firm performance. Vertical consensus among middle managers and executives was most critical for firm performance.

Other studies have shown similar results.[62] An early study examined the impact of organizational alignment on financial performance. The researcher used surveys from 113 senior managers in the furniture and apparel industry reporting directly to their CEO.[63] The authors found a strong correlation between alignment and financial performance based on a subjective assessment of the firms' sales, profitability, and overall growth. A more recent study analyzing data from 156 marketing, manufacturing, and R&D managers showed higher interdepartmental integration improved product development and product management performance. The researchers used level of communication and exchange of standardized, documented information among departments to measure interdepartmental integration.

In 2020, scholars investigated the importance of manager alignment and commitment to company strategy for eventual success.[64] They obtained information about 164 manager-subordinate relationships from two companies' human resources databases. They surveyed the managers about their commitment to their firm's strategy plan, as well as their perceptions of strategy consensus in the company. They also surveyed the subordinate team members about their commitment to the firm's strategy. The researchers found a positive correlation between the managers' perceptions of strategy consensus and their own commitment to the strategy plan. They also found a positive correlation between the managers' own commitment to their company's strategy plan and the subordinates' commitment to the plan. The positive relationship was strengthened when the managers felt they were more aligned with the CEO's vision for the company. Thus, the companies' success depended on alignment between leadership and middle management on strategy execution.

Many companies' strategy planning processes hinder consensus and alignment. Companies in which executives not only become enamored of internally focused pet projects, but also underestimate the importance of middle and frontline employees, suffer most. Visualize a firm with a large number of strategy initiatives, each internally focused and based on an executive's intuitive leaps. Because personnel do not agree on the conclusions drawn, it is difficult to achieve consensus among senior executives, between senior executives and middle management, and among divisions.

A lack of consensus sometimes occurs due to the abstract and pithy nature of a company's mission statement. GE's value of "imagination at work," for example, provided cover for inwardly focused initiatives that sowed discord among units and divisions.[65] In other companies, senior executives use the budget process, their influence with CEOs, and other approaches to gain approval and resources for their projects. Typically, the executives justify the projects using internal criteria narrowly based on measurable factors, such as efficiency and cash flow. Further, the justification is based on intuitive leaps, mythical numbers, and salient claims. Without strategy consensus on externally facing criteria, the internal focus and discord grow. Over time, corporate budgeting becomes a political minefield, with managers creating new initiatives to grab more of the resource pie but pitching them as being aligned with abstract criteria.

7.7 Inhibitor 7: Decoupled Measurement and Diffuse Accountability

Imagine having a fever and going to a physician. The doctor prescribes a fever-reducing pill and tells you to take as many as you want.

Why do doctors prescribe measured doses? Why do they take a patient's temperature rather than simply ask if he or she has a fever or not? Why do they try to find the cause of the fever? In medical practice, the inputs (medicine), throughputs (fever causes), and outputs (fever reduction) are measurably coupled. Doctors quantify the importance of inputs in determining an outcome. They use a science-based approach to determine importance weights. That is, they not only know acetaminophen reduces fever, but also know the underlying relationship between a specific acetaminophen dosage, how and why it acts on the body, and how much it reduces fever. Further, physicians know they should prescribe different treatments for bacterial and viral infections. Knowing the relative importance of the two inputs is critical to managing the output. By quantifying the nature and magnitude of the association between inputs, mediators, and outputs, physicians know what will happen when they prescribe medicine. They do not rely on salience or mythical numbers and have no need for intuitive leaps when treating patients.

The strategy process for many companies does not provide clear mechanisms. The process does not identify inputs and outputs, measure them, nor ascertain the relative weights of key inputs in determining a desired outcome. Their measurement is almost always decoupled, and executives consistently use intuitive leaps and salience to guess the inputs. Because the association between the inputs and the outputs is unknown, executives often overshoot or undershoot their goals. Yet, they continue gathering data on increasing numbers of metrics and subjectively pick and choose from them to justify their actions. The CEOs interviewed in Chap. 2 clearly identified the lack of an empirical link between initiatives and outcomes as a shortcoming of the strategy process. The CEOs said their senior executives made the error because they relied on expensive, siloed research of broad industry or market trends not applicable to their company.

EPCO executives sought to optimize their strategy initiatives. They agreed their relevant output was profitability and their inputs were the many existing initiatives. Yet, the executives lacked a statistically valid approach to quantifying the relative contribution of each initiative to profitability. Over time, each executive gathered different metrics. For project management alone, the company developed more than 300 metrics. But not a single senior executive reviewed more than 30 metrics. Each saw a unique set. When asked how the metrics were related or affected outcomes like project profitability, each executive made an intuitive leap—"it's obvious doing X will lead to higher Y." Or the executive had no idea about the correlation between the metrics—"how much of a change in X can we expect for a unit change in Y?" In the end, the executives insisted every metric should be retained. The process led to intense discord among executives, even as they all agreed on the objective of increased profitability.

Decoupled measurement typically results from senior executives' reliance on metric averages or percentages taken from industry or market trends. The data provide mythical numbers but preclude executives from statistically determining the magnitude of individual initiatives' correlation to outcomes. Returning to the medical analogy, it is not enough for physicians to know the level of a patient's fever and the medicine to prescribe. The physician must understand the association between them—how much the fever declines for each dose of medicine. The concept is simple to understand but difficult to implement in companies because it requires the strategy process to fully embrace (1) the measurement of metrics related to inputs, throughputs, and outputs; (2) building the statistical capability needed to determine the association between metrics; and (3) prioritizing activities based on their importance, rather than salience.

Senior executives at SCHOOLCO cited students' low academic scores and decided to make "higher investments in more extracurricular activities to attain better academic achievement." Yet, the executives did not develop a statistical linkage between extracurricular activities and academic performance. They failed to answer a simple question: How much improvement in academic performance can be expected for every unit increase in extracurricular activity investment? SCHOOLCO knew only the averages of both metrics and used them to draw conclusions about their relative importance (see Fig. 7.4, Panel A). SCHOOLCO failed to couple the metrics, that is, examine the correlation or association between them using statistical analysis (see Fig. 7.4, Panel B). Without coupling the metrics, senior executives at the district were unable to determine the importance of extracurricular activities in driving academic performance.

When initiatives and metrics are decoupled from an agreed-upon outcome, executives collect as many metrics as possible, hoping some or one of them will be accepted. The approach to strategy planning leads to diffuse accountability. Despite being responsible for specific metrics, no one is accountable for the final outcome. A classic study showed many companies measured and rewarded "A" while hoping for "B."[66] A university in the study offered

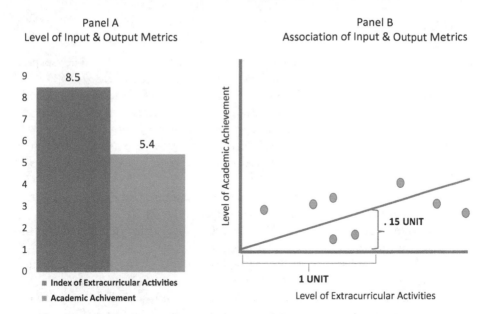

Panel A
Level of Input & Output Metrics

Panel B
Association of Input & Output Metrics

■ Index of Extracurricular Activities
■ Academic Achivement

Level of Extracurricular Activities

Fig. 7.4 Decoupled metrics at SCHOOLCO

teaching awards to drive high-quality research. An oil and gas company rewarded employees for sustainability initiatives, while senior executives wanted to increase profits through hydraulic fracturing equipment sales. One company suffered from low levels of customer satisfaction and market share due to late delivery. Senior executives, meanwhile, emphasized product quality. The statistical association between customer satisfaction and delivery time was higher than between customer satisfaction and product quality. Once senior executives recognized the relative importance of the two strategy areas, they created an incentive system to reward on-time deliveries and metrics to monitor late deliveries. Within two quarters, the company increased sales and margins by 22% and cut customer churn in half.

7.8 Conclusion

The inhibitors riddling the strategy planning processes do not reflect inherent weaknesses of senior executives. Nor can executives eliminate them by being aware of their existence or by becoming more thoughtful. Rather, they require systemic and systematic changes in the strategy planning process and the general approach senior executives take to it. Senior executives can blunt the frustrations of strategy inhibitors and make their strategy process robust by implementing strategy enablers described in the next chapter.

Notes

1. Combs, Barbara, and Paul Slovic (1979), "Causes of death: Biased newspaper coverage and biased judgments," *Journalism Quarterly*, 56(4), 837–843.
2. Lichtenstein, Sarah, Paul Slovic, Baruch Fischhoff, Mark Layman, and Barbara Combs (1978), "Judged frequency of lethal events," *Journal of Experimental Psychology: Human Learning and Memory*, 4(6), 551.
3. Bateman, Thomas S., and Carl P. Zeithaml (1989), "The psychological context of strategic decisions: A model and convergent experimental findings," *Strategic Management Journal* 10(1), 59–74.
4. Schwenk, Charles R. (1984), "Cognitive simplification processes in strategic decision-making," *Strategic Management Journal*, 5(2), 111–128.
5. Lovallo, Dan P., and Olivier Sibony (2006), "Distortions and deceptions in strategic decisions," *McKinsey Quarterly*, 18.

    Schwenk, Charles R., (1984), "Cognitive simplification processes in strategic decision-making," *Strategic Management Journal*, 5(2), 111–128.
6. Mittal, Vikas, Jules Rosen, and Carrie Leana (2009), "A dual-driver model of retention and turnover in the direct care workforce," *The Gerontologist*, 49(5), 623–634.

    Rosen, Jules, Emily M. Stiehl, Vikas Mittal, and Carrie R. Leana (2001), "Stayers, leavers, and switchers among certified nursing assistants in nursing homes: A longitudinal investigation of turnover intent, staff retention, and turnover," *The Gerontologist*, 51(5), 597–609.
7. Miller, C. Chet, and R. Duane Ireland (2005), "Intuition in strategic decision making: friend or foe in the fast-paced 21st century?" *Academy of Management Perspectives*, 19(1), 19–30.
8. Miller, C. Chet, and R. Duane Ireland (2005), "Intuition in strategic decision making: friend or foe in the fast-paced 21st century?" *Academy of Management Perspectives*, 19(1), 19–30.
9. Schwenk, Charles R. (1988), "The cognitive perspective on strategic decision making," *Journal of Management Studies*, 25(1), 41–55.
10. Jonas, Eva, Stefan Schulz-Hardt, Dieter Frey, and Norman Thelen (2001), "Confirmation bias in sequential information search after preliminary decisions: an expansion of dissonance theoretical research on selective exposure to information," *Journal of Personality and Social Psychology*, 80(4), 557.
11. Kenny, David A. (2008). "Reflections on mediation," *Organizational Research Methods*, 11(2), 353–358.
12. Klemm, Mary, Stuart Sanderson, and George Luffman (1991), "Mission statements: Selling corporate values to employees," *Long Range Planning*, 24(3), 73–78.
13. Bart, Christopher K. (1997), "Industrial firms and the power of mission," *Industrial Marketing Management*, 26(4), 371–38.

14. Singer, Max (1971), "The vitality of mythical numbers," *The Public Interest*, 23, 3.
15. "Digitalisation and Energy," IEA Report, November 2017. Available at: https://www.iea.org/reports/digitalisation-and-energy,   Last   accessed: September 2020.
16. Pemberton, Chris (2016), "Gartner CMO Spend Survey 2016–2017 shows marketing budgets continue to climb," *Weekly Newsletter, Gartner*. Available at: https://www.gartner.com/en/marketing/insights/articles/gartner-cmo-spend-survey-2016-2017-shows-marketing-budgets-continue-to-climb, Last accessed: September 2020.
17. Jonas, Eva, Stefan Schulz-Hardt, Dieter Frey, and Norman Thelen (2001), "Confirmation bias in sequential information search after preliminary decisions: an expansion of dissonance theoretical research on selective exposure to information," *Journal of Personality and Social Psychology*, 80(4), 557–571.
18. Khashimova, Katherine (2020), "Protesters decry Amazon warehouse conditions as commerce giant gears up for holiday shopping blitz," *The Spokesman-Review*, Saturday, November. https://www.spokesman.com/stories/2020/nov/27/protesters-decry-amazon-warehouse-conditions-as-co/, Last accessed: December 2020.
19. Ward, Bronagh, Vittoria Bufalari, Mark Tulay, Sara E. Murphy (2020), "COVID-19 and inequality: A test of corporate purpose," Test of Corporate Purpose, KKS Advisors. Available at: COVID-19 and Inequality: A Test of Corporate Purpose (harvard.edu), Last accessed: December 2020.
20. Hall, Stephen, Dan Lovallo, and Reinier Musters (2012), "How to put your money where your strategy is," *McKinsey Quarterly*, March, 1–11.
21. Arkes, Hal R., and Catherine Blumer (1985), "The psychology of sunk cost," *Organizational Behavior and Human Decision Processes*, 35(1), 124–140.
    Garland, Howard (1990). "Throwing good money after bad: The effect of sunk costs on the decision to escalate commitment to an ongoing project," *Journal of Applied Psychology*, 75(6), 728–731.
22. Boulding, William, Ruskin Morgan, and Richard Staelin (1997), "Pulling the plug to stop the new product drain," *Journal of Marketing Research*, 34(1), 164–176.
23. Sleesman, Dustin J., Donald E. Conlon, Gerry McNamara, and Jonathan E. Miles (2012), "Cleaning up the big muddy: A meta-analytic review of the determinants of escalation of commitment," *Academy of Management Journal*, 55(3), 541–562.
    Roth, Stefan, Thomas Robbert, and Lennart Straus (2015), "On the sunk-cost effect in economic decision-making: a meta-analytic review," *Business Research*, 8(1), 99–138.
24. Alba, Joseph W., and J. Wesley Hutchinson (1987), "Dimensions of consumer expertise," *Journal of Consumer Research*, 13(4), 411–454.

25. Hartman, Raymond S., Michael J. Doane, and Chi-Keung Woo (1991), "Consumer rationality and the status quo," *The Quarterly Journal of Economics*, 106(1), 141–162.

26. Kahneman, Daniel, Jack L. Knetsch, and Richard H. Thaler (1991), "Anomalies: The endowment effect, loss aversion, and status quo bias," *Journal of Economic Perspectives*, 5(1), 193–206.

27. Arkes, Hal R., and Catherine Blumer (1985). "The psychology of sunk cost," *Organizational Behavior and Human Decision Processes*, 35(1), 124–140.

28. McGlothlin, William H. (1956), "Stability of choices among uncertain alternatives," *The American Journal of Psychology*, 69(4), 604–615.

29. Samuelson, William, and Richard Zeckhauser (1988), "Status quo bias in decision making," *Journal of Risk and Uncertainty*, 1(1), 7–59.

30. Bowman, Edward H. (1982), "Risk seeking by troubled firms," *Sloan Management Review (pre-1986)* 23(4), Summer, 33.

31. Pfeffer, Jeffrey, and Gerald R. Salancik (2003), *The external control of organizations: A resource dependence perspective*, Stanford University Press.

32. Hillman, Amy J., Michael C. Withers, and Brian J. Collins (2009), "Resource dependence theory: A review," *Journal of Management* 35(6), 1404–1427.

33. Friedman, Milton (2013), *Why government is the problem*, Hoover Press.

34. James L. Payne (1991), "Why Congress can't kick the tax and spend habit," *Imprimis (Hillsdale College)*, 20(5), May.

35. Buehler, Roger, Dale Griffin, and Michael Ross (1994), "Exploring the 'planning fallacy': Why people underestimate their task completion times," *Journal of Personality and Social Psychology*, 67(3), 366–381.

    Kahneman, Daniel, and Dan Lovallo (1993), "Timid choices and bold forecasts: A cognitive perspective on risk taking," *Management Science*, 39(1), 17–31.

36. Bent, Flyvbjerg (2008), "Curbing optimism bias and strategic misrepresentation in planning: Reference class forecasting in practice," *European Planning Studies*, 16(1), 3–21.

37. Gryta, Thomas, and Ted Mann (2018), "GE powered the American century—Then it burned out," *Wall Street Journal*, December 14.

38. Berger, Philip G., and Eli Ofek (1995), "Diversification's effect on firm value," *Journal of Financial Economics*, 37(1), 39–65.

39. Lang, Larry HP, and Rene M. Stulz (1994), "Tobin's q, corporate diversification, and firm performance," *Journal of Political Economy*, 102(6), 1248–1280.

40. He, Xin, and Vikas Mittal (2007), "The effect of decision risk and project stage on escalation of commitment," *Organizational Behavior and Human Decision Processes*, 103(2), 225–237.

41. Hill, Andrew (2016), "Strategic quitting and when to pull the plug on a failed project," *Financial Times*, May 9.

42. Hall, Stephen, Dan Lovallo, and Reinier Musters (2012), "How to put your money where your strategy is," *McKinsey Quarterly*, March, 1–11.

43. Mittal, Vikas, Shrihari Sridhar, and Roger Best (2020). "To cut costs, know your customers," *MIT Sloan Management Review*, Reprint #62212.
44. Kahn, Barbara E. (1995), "Consumer variety-seeking among goods and services: An integrative review," 139, *Wharton Faculty Research*, University of Pennsylvania, Scholarly Commons.
45. Gist, Marilyn E. (1987), "Self-efficacy: Implications for organizational behavior and human resource management," *Academy of Management Review*, 12(3), 472–485.
46. Mittal, Vikas, William T. Ross Jr., and Michael Tsiros (2002), "The role of issue valence and issue capability in determining effort investment," *Journal of Marketing Research*, 39(4), 455–468.
47. Papenhausen, Chris (2006), "Half full or half empty: The effects of top managers' dispositional optimism on strategic decision-making and firm performance," *Journal of Behavioral & Applied Management*, 7(2), 104–115.
48. Schoar, Antoinette (2002), "Effects of corporate diversification on productivity," *The Journal of Finance*, 57(6), 2379–2403.
    Best, Ronald W., Charles W. Hodges, and Bing-Xuan Lin (2004), "Does information asymmetry explain the diversification discount?" *Journal of Financial Research*, 27(2), 235–249.
    Choe, Chongwoo, and Xiangkang Yin (2009), "Diversification discount, information rents, and internal capital markets," *The Quarterly Review of Economics and Finance*, 49(2), 178–196.
49. Botti, Simona, and Sheena S. Iyengar (2006), "The dark side of choice: When choice impairs social welfare," *Journal of Public Policy & Marketing*, 25(1), 24–38.
50. Sethi-Iyengar, Sheena, Gur Huberman, and Wei Jiang ((2004), "How much choice is too much? Contributions to 401 (k) retirement plans," *Pension Design and Structure: New Lessons from Behavioral Finance*, 83, 84–87.
51. Iyengar, Sheena S., and Emir Kamenica (2010). "Choice proliferation, simplicity seeking, and asset allocation," *Journal of Public Economics*, 94(7–8), 530–539.
52. Mittal, Vikas, and Carly Frennea (2010), "Customer satisfaction: a strategic review and guidelines for managers," *MSI Fast Forward Series, Marketing Science Institute*, Cambridge, MA.
53. "For Wells Fargo, culture change is a tough sell," *Insurancenewswire.com*, March 17, 2019. https://insurancenewsnet.com/oarticle/for-wells-fargo-culture-change-is-a-tough-sell#.XJrQUI3rsqM, Last accessed December 20, 2020.
54. Krantz, Matt (2016), "Wells Fargo gets hit where it hurts: No longer most valuable," USA Today, September 14. https://www.usatoday.com/story/money/markets/2016/09/14/wells-fargo-gets-hit-where-hurts/90325728/, Last accessed December 20, 2020.

55. Langer, Ellen J. (1975), "The illusion of control," *Journal of Personality and Social Psychology*, 32(2), 311–328.

56. Gollwitzer, Peter M., and Ronald F. Kinney (1989), "Effects of deliberative and implemental mind-sets on illusion of control," *Journal of Personality and Social Psychology*, 56(4), 531–542.

57. Krueger Jr., Norris, and Peter R. Dickson (1994), "How believing in ourselves increases risk taking: Perceived self-efficacy and opportunity recognition," *Decision Sciences*, 25(3), 385–400.

   Mittal, Vikas, William T. Ross Jr, and Michael Tsiros (2002), "The role of issue valence and issue capability in determining effort investment," *Journal of Marketing Research*, 39(4), 455–468.

58. Durand, Rodolphe (2003), "Predicting a firm's forecasting ability: The roles of organizational illusion of control and organizational attention," *Strategic Management Journal*, 24(9), 821–838.

59. Knight, Don, Craig L. Pearce, Ken G. Smith, Judy D. Olian, Henry P. Sims, Ken A. Smith, and Patrick Flood (1999), "Top management team diversity, group process, and strategic consensus," *Strategic Management Journal*, 20(5), 445–465.

60. Homburg, Christian, Harley Krohmer, and John P. Workman. Jr. (1999), "Strategic consensus and performance: The role of strategy type and market-related dynamism," *Strategic Management Journal*, 20(4), 339–357.

61. Kellermanns, Franz W., Jorge Walter, Steven W. Floyd, Christoph Lechner, and John C. Shaw (2011), "To agree or not to agree? A meta-analytical review of strategic consensus and organizational performance," *Journal of Business Research*, 64(2), 126–133.

62. Kathuria, Ravi, Maheshkumar P. Joshi, and Stephen J. Porth (2007), "Organizational alignment and performance: past, present and future," *Management Decision*, 45(3), 503–517.

63. Powell, Thomas C. (1992), "Organizational alignment as competitive advantage," *Strategic Management Journal*, 13(2), 119–134.

64. Ateş, Nüfer Yasin, Murat Tarakci, Jeanine Pieternel Porck, Daan van Knippenberg, and Patrick J.F. Groenen (2020), "The dark side of visionary leadership in strategy implementation: Strategic alignment, strategic consensus, and commitment," *Journal of Management*, 46(5), 637–665.

65. "Charting GE's historic rise and tortured downfall," Bloomberg, January 30 2019. See: https://www.bloomberg.com/graphics/2019-general-electric-rise-and-downfall/, Last accessed December 20, 2020.

66. Kerr, Steven (1975), "On the folly of rewarding A, while hoping for B," *Academy of Management Journal*, 18(4), 769–783.

8

Strategy Planning Enablers

We want you to devote a lot of your time and energy and company resources to a process that will identify a large number of initiatives to distract upper, middle, and frontline employees. It should not meet the CEO's expectations of clarity and focus from the strategy planning process. Oh, and by the way, implementing the process should have a negative, zero, or barely perceptible positive effect on the company's financial performance. On the upside, it will make everyone believe they are working toward a goal, even though the company lacks any objective, statistical evidence about the process, underlying initiatives, or company performance.

When the hypothetical directive above was given to dozens of senior executives, not a single one agreed to implement the process. Yet, as described in Chap. 2, virtually all CEOs want the strategy process to include fewer biases, politics, and conflicts, and more focus and relevance.

Many senior executives and managers believe strategy planning improves their company's bottom-line. However, strategy planning has almost no impact on companies' financial performance, with 79% of studies showing a negative or zero association.

Many CEOs believe their company is not reaping the benefits of strategy planning. Still, they do not believe the process is a nuisance or symbolic activity.[1] They believe it is necessary, whether done systematically or on an emergent basis, and that it can be improved considerably.[2]

Chapter 7 identifies a set of seven inhibitors impeding senior executives from realizing the positive financial benefits of strategy planning. The

© The Author(s), under exclusive license to Springer Nature Switzerland AG 2021
V. Mittal, S. Sridhar, *Focus*, https://doi.org/10.1007/978-3-030-70720-0_8

inhibitors are systemic, pervasive, and deeply ingrained in the strategy planning process of many companies. But simply alerting executives to the inhibitors' existence does not ameliorate their ill-effects. For chain restaurant group FOODCO (see Chap. 1 for a full description), attempts to alert the owner that the company relied on salience, and ignored customer needs, to make intuitive leaps did not change its strategy planning behavior. At TOOLCO, also described in Chap. 1, asking division leaders to reduce initiatives led them to add another initiative as a way to reduce initiatives. At SCHOOLCO, senior executives extolled the virtue of strategy focus but clamored for more investments in failing initiatives to expand their personal resource base and influence.

In all cases, the executives were smart, well-meaning, and committed to using the strategy planning process to improve their organization's performance. In all cases, the usual approach of combat-and-conquer that made the executive the main source of the change-management process failed. Providing senior executives with personalized coaching to make them aware of their biases, sending them to continuing-education programs, providing more information, or believing in their own self-improvement tools also failed. As one senior executive said, "I've done dozens of these self-assessments and been told the same thing multiple times. It does not work."

Surveyed CEOs have described many cases in which providing more information does not improve strategy planning. Strategy planning success is not based on an extensive information system. Simply capturing more data and adding capacity to analyze it does not improve the process. In fact, CEOs have said a surfeit of reports commissioned by different functional executives create analysis paralysis during strategy planning. More information can inundate but not necessarily illuminate strategy decision-making.

Many executives and managers agree with CEOs that strategy inhibitors are pervasive. But their plans for addressing the inhibitors center around an all-too-familiar trope: they can avoid the deleterious consequences if they understand the inhibitors and are mindful of them. Conversations with dozens of CEOs who understand their company's strategy inhibitors indicated they tried to resolve them through leadership training and educating their executives. Many developed their own leadership training programs designed to teach values, missions, and decision-biases to senior management. Not a single one was able to improve the company's strategy planning process. Rather, the programs acted much like a placebo. After the leadership training, executives reported being more cognizant of the inhibitors and developing plans to address them. But their new strategy planning processes did not have a positive effect on company performance.

Simply put, the seven primary strategy planning inhibitors must be addressed using a broad approach going beyond awareness, leadership training, and executive coaching. Companies must put in place specific systems and processes to "un-inhibit" the inhibitors and replace them with enablers that make the strategy planning process a positive catalyst for focus and improved financial performance.

8.1 Enabler 1: Chain-link Your Strategy Map

Strategy planning at its core is the process of linking different inputs to throughputs and desired outputs. The linking process requires senior executives to agree on critical inputs, throughputs, and outputs and how they should be measured, then use a systematic, statistical process to understand their relationship. The chain-linked map of a company's strategy can be visualized as a box-and-arrows diagram, where each arrow represents the linkage between an input and its outcome. Panel B in Figure 7.2 (see Chap. 7) is an example of a strategy map.

A formal chain-linked strategy map links all inputs, throughputs, and outputs. The inputs are a company's resources, activities, and initiatives conducted and managed by different senior executives. Senior executives typically control the inputs though the department, function, region, division, or market they lead. Throughputs are the activities of key stakeholders (primarily customers) that link to cash flows. The primary throughput for a company's strategy is customer value and loyalty, including word-of-mouth activity, recommendations, and repurchase behavior. The strategy output important to CEOs, board members, and shareholders can be measured as cash flow, revenue, sales, and stock market performance.

The process of formally chain-linking a company's strategy involves multiple steps. First, executives develop a common understanding of key inputs, throughputs, and outputs. Second, they agree on the specific measures and metrics to be used. The metrics can be operational (e.g., manufacturing, operations), financial (e.g., accounting, sales, finance), or customer-based (e.g., customer surveys, sales). Third, executives and analysts agree on the different linkages among the constructs and statistically determine their strength. For example, consider the vice president of HR at a major company. The executive's critical inputs might include employee training and compensation, which should lead to higher engagement. The throughput is customer value, as the executive believes engaged employees can better satisfy customer needs. Improved customer value should lead to increased sales and company stock price, which are set as the critical outputs. Similar chain-links could be developed for departments like sales, marketing, manufacturing, and finance.

Formally chain-linking a company's strategy produces three important insights not available from the traditional strategy planning processes detailed in Chaps. 4, 5, and 6. First, it forces executives to clarify and agree on the components of their strategy. Listing the strategy constructs and their measures can be a meaningful first step for senior executives to begin the alignment process. Second, it enables executives to articulate the possible linkages among the inputs, throughputs, and outputs and bring clarity and specificity to their organization's strategy. For example, the vice president of HR may propose a link between employee engagement and customer satisfaction. The vice president of marketing may propose a link between brand strength and customer satisfaction. And the vice president of manufacturing may propose a link between quality control and customer satisfaction. The executives must agree on the constructs' metrics and quantify them across customers, regions, clients, and other units of interest. Third and most importantly, the process forces executives to quantify each linkage for a precise and complete picture of their strategy map. By quantifying the linkages, executives can understand the relative strength of their strategy inputs and rank them from the strongest to the weakest. They can then build strategy around the strongest linkages, ignoring the inputs with little to no effect on critical outcomes.

Panel A in Figure 7.2 (see Chap. 7) shows a nursing home group's strategy, which relied on intuitive leaps and salience to represent reality. Panel B in Figure 7.2 shows a chain-linked strategy for understanding employees and decreasing turnover. Once the nursing home's strategy was chain-linked, executives could clearly complete the following objectives:

- Identify the components of the strategy map. Rather than focusing only on higher pay, the company's executives identified and agreed on health insurance, promotion opportunities, employee age, and higher pay as inputs affecting the throughput of employees' turnover intentions. They agreed the final outcome of interest would be actual employee turnover. Further, they agreed on the metrics to represent each of the strategy map components. For example, they measured employee turnover as the percentage of employees who voluntarily left the nursing home over an 18-month period. Discussions about defining the strategy components and their metrics ensured each executive developed deep understanding of the map and a commitment to using it.
- Quantify the strength of each link in the strategy map. The nursing home executives statistically quantified the association of each input with the

throughput turnover intentions. This enabled executives to prioritize their focus on the input with the greatest association with the outcome of interest. Prior to building the strategy map, the executives did not know the strength of association between the inputs, throughputs, and outputs and relied on salience, gut feel, industry studies, and leaps of faith.

- Focus and sequence their work by prioritizing the most important inputs and minimizing the rest. The executives focused their effort on providing healthcare and promotion opportunities and agreed to de-prioritize higher pay. The approach allowed them to achieve more by doing less and provide clarity to the company CEO and other stakeholders.

Chain-linking strategy components using statistical models removes subjectivity, bias, conflict, and politics. It increases the objectivity of strategy planning, using all the available data and information, and ensures it can be verified against industry norms. Failing to chain-link strategy components increases executives' reliance on salience and intuitive leaps, which leads to excessive initiatives and makes it harder to focus and sequence strategy priorities. Critically, without chain-linking strategy inputs, throughputs, and outputs, executives cannot determine each input's relative importance. Instead, they rely on gut feeling and salience as a proxy.

8.2 Enabler 2: Know the Give-Get of Each Link

Senior executives often lead strategy astray by basing their actions on their gut feelings and beliefs. The intuitions typically reflect salience, not the underlying importance of a strategy factor. Strategy factor importance denotes the give and get relationship between an input (the strategy factor) and an output (the desired outcome).

FOODCO's owner consistently focused on food quality and ignored the factor's give-get relationship with sales. The give-get was zero. That is, no matter how much the owner gave in terms of food quality, he would get zero lift in sales. Extensive parking and fast service were shown to achieve a corresponding lift in sales. But FOODCO's owner was beguiled by food quality's salience because the company lacked a statistically valid quantification of the give-get relationships.

In most strategy planning processes, quantifying the give-get of each input is relatively simple. The difficult part is convincing executives to let go of their preconceived notions—their salience bias and leaps of faith—to embrace the science-based evidence. Even when the give-get of each strategy map linkage is clear, many executives maintain their original beliefs. They lack the humility to embrace science-based evidence. FOODCO's owner lacked the humility and commitment necessary to use the give-get scores of food quality relative to other inputs. Relying on prior experience, executives ignore important strategy elements and create superfluous initiatives, value-added waste, and confusion. Executives taking the time to understand and internalize the give-get scores of different inputs are able to let go of unimportant initiatives. The executives can turn their companies around by recalibrating their strategy focus.

How do senior executives know they are basing their company's strategy on give-get scores and not mistaking salience for importance? The give-get scores should only be statistically determined using data from different company units, such as customers, branches, and employees. They cannot be intuited or configured without data and statistical analysis. Decades of research shows statistical models are more robust than human experts at capturing and quantifying the association of multiple inputs to an output.[3] In one study, experts on a doctoral program admissions committee used inputs like grade point averages and test scores to select students. When it was time to predict the students' success years later, researchers compared the experts' predictions to those of a simple statistical model using the same inputs. The model more accurately predicted student success than the members of the admissions committee and professors did. The simple statistical model combined the inputs in an unbiased manner. The human experts, on the other hand, incorporated their idiosyncrasies and biases when combining inputs and outputs.

A quantified give-get score can also be converted to an input-output ratio. For example, a 10% increase in food quality (the input) might be expected to induce a 3% increase in sales. But without statistical analysis, no intuition or judgment can quantify the input-output linkage. To test their knowledge of each linkage's give-get, executives can engage in a thought exercise. Suppose a company CEO wants to improve revenues by 10% and margins by 5%. Senior executives can use give-get scores of various linkages to identify and prioritize the inputs with the highest impact on throughputs (like customer satisfaction) and outputs (like sales and margins). Rather than justifying initiatives based on salience or intuitive leaps, executives must make credible if-then statements based on the give-get of each strategy input.

8.3   Enabler 3: Achieve More by Doing Less

Strategy planning fosters a tendency to do more—more projects, more initiatives—to improve performance. CEO's complain their senior executives are unable to use strategy planning to focus and sequence the work of their employees. Initiatives and projects pile on because executives cannot prioritize them based on their relative impact on a common, agreed-upon outcome.

To achieve more by doing less, a company's strategy planning process must embrace system-wide data collection on initiatives and projects. The firm must then analyze the data using advanced statistical models to link inputs, throughputs, and outputs. The process cannot be accomplished using reports from consultants that summarize industries, markets, or macro trends. Such reports fail to understand the intricate reality of individual companies and lack the granular data needed to develop chain-linked strategy maps.

Thus, an executive team may have four different projects on safety, employee engagement, on-time delivery, and customer communication. Each project may have different success metrics, making it difficult to compare them. If the executive team can link the metrics to a throughput predicting a higher-level outcome (e.g., sales or margins), the team can use the relative importance measures to prioritize and rank the projects. In other words, an objective methodology complementing the give-get approach removes bias, politics, personal preferences, and salience from the task of ranking initiatives. The objective methodology uses the give-get score to rank the initiatives from most effective to least effective. Rather than engaging in endless arguments, politics, persuasion, and debates, executives can devote their time to maximizing the outcome and impact of the most important initiatives. They can achieve more by doing less.

The Superintendent at a large school district used the methodology to cut strategy initiatives from more than 200 to fewer than 20, pare down grants that could not be linked to academic achievement or student safety, and provide school principals time to work on the basics. The results were a decrease in achievement gap, improved academic scores, reduced disciplinary placements, more students taking the SAT, and improved SAT scores, among others. In SCHOOLCO (see Chap. 1 for description), the superintendent wanted to do more to help students and was reluctant to prioritize initiatives based on a systematic comparison. Over two years, the district continued to add initiatives and do more even as performance declined across the board. Principals grew weary and senior executives continued to support their favored initiatives using cherry-picked data. One official cited a student winning a spelling bee contest as proof the school had turned around through its reading program. Yet, no demonstrable link between the reading program and academic achievement could be established.

8.4 Enabler 4: Relentlessly Implement the Not-To-Do List

Effective strategy planning enables executives to focus and sequence their work by highlighting the most important inputs. The focus on prioritized inputs—strategy areas, initiatives, and activities—improves customer value, drives revenue and sales, and lowers costs. Many executives deploy more resources to prioritized areas. They are rarely successful at de-emphasizing, reducing, or eliminating low priority areas.

Unsuccessful strategy plans try to find more and more resources for high priority initiatives and activities. More successful plans redeploy resources from low-priority areas to high-priority areas. The strategy has three benefits. First, it slowly weeds out low-priority initiatives, focusing and sequencing executives' attention on important initiatives. Second, it simplifies strategy and its implementation. Third, it provides clarity and focus to middle-management and frontline employees.

Almost every strategy plan and senior executive has a to-do list designed to help teams focus on the items deemed most important. A better list would be a not-to-do list based on activities, initiatives, and strategy factors with zero association with desired outcomes. Simply by jettisoning the activities and doing less, executives can achieve more. Thus, identifying factors not associated with desired outcomes is as—if not more—critical than prioritizing factors highly associated with the outcome. In statistical parlance, the process entails identifying and de-prioritizing statistically nonsignificant factors, or factors with a zero give-get score.

EPCO (see Chap. 1 for a full description) was unable to prioritize prospects for bidding and struggled to develop an order intake forecast. The firm historically hired an increasing number of salespeople to bid on more jobs. Once the CEO understood the discrepancy between EPCO's order intake forecasts and actual bookings, he charged his senior sales executive with developing a not-to-bid list, i.e., a list of prospects to ignore because of poor business fit or low bid-win probability. By bidding on fewer projects and diverting resources from wasted bids, the sales executive ensured timely and higher-quality bids. Loss aversion, the status quo, and sunk costs—all inhibitors discussed in Chap. 7—were eliminated. The not-to-bid list enabled the group to develop strategy focus and improve performance.

For strategy planning, making a not-to-do list can be more valuable than making a to-do list. For example, EPCO's senior sales executive used the process to overcome many strategy inhibitors. First, due to loss aversion, many salespeople did not want to give up prospects to which they had devoted significant time. Second, many salespeople considered maintaining the status quo as less painful personally than the uncertainty and upheaval of change. Third, the salespeople exhibited optimism bias, especially for newer prospects. They continued to pursue all prospects, optimistic they would win them in the future. Fourth, the process of letting prospects go was fraught with negative emotions, especially for salespeople who had invested personal capital and resources into the relationships.

Making a credible and useful not-to-do list requires a system able to quantify the relative importance of projects based on inputs and outputs. Executives must also agree on two cut-offs to split the projects into three groups: "Definitely-to-do," "maybe-should-do," and "not-to-do." The executives must finally agree what percentage of the projects must fall in each group. Otherwise, each executive will at least want his or her project in the maybe-should-do list. Recall ExxonMobil CEO Lee Raymond required his corporate planning team to identify 3% to 5% of the company's assets for potential disposal every year.[4] Even if the percent or number of projects to be eliminated is small, the process can set a precedent and help executives institute a culture of cleaning up and moving on.

EPCO developed its not-to-bid list using machine-learning algorithms to identify patterns among the company's historical bidding pipeline. Reviewing the total pipeline, executives saw clear patterns based on size, region, and client type. The machine learning algorithm identified with 80% certainty the type of prospects the company would always win and always lose. Once the losing prospects had been identified, EPCO simply had to ignore them. Previously, the company bid indiscriminately on every prospect, straining the business development team. The not-to-bid list took gut feeling and intuition out of the process. The results were reduced costs per bid and improved bid quality. The cost of business development and bidding decreased, while the amount of business won increased, much to the sales director's surprise.

8.5   Enabler 5: Flip the Planning Template

Most strategy planning processes follow a template that puts the cart before the horse. In some companies, the chief financial officer decides on a sales forecast and other executives create a list of activities to achieve it. In other companies, values drive activities. Starting with a goal—numerical or subjective—senior executives add color and resolution to make it come alive and only then follow through with metrics and budget numbers to justify it. The template is usually a classification schematic—a way to classify different spends, activities, and resources. The classification buckets can be based on functions (e.g., HR, finance, marketing, operations, and sales), regions (e.g., North, East, and South) or business lines. They are rarely based on strategy areas driving customer value.

The typical strategy planning template illustrates the common CEO lament in Chap. 2. Namely, the strategy process is unrelated to customer value and internally focused. The template must therefore be flipped to start with customer value, the strongest predictor of a company's financial performance, including cash flow.[5] Then, executives can identify strategy areas that drive customer value and create a chain-linked strategy map.[6]

At FACILITYCO, each division and regional leader provided a budget, profit-and-loss statement, and list of initiatives. The initiatives were typically based on senior executives' understanding of key issues based on conversations with customers and employees. At coatings and abrasives firm ABCO, the template consisted of four buckets—employees, technology, customers, and finance—to classify activities and set goals. The goals were based on senior executives' intuition, which relied on conversations with employees, customers, and consultants. ABCO had no measurement-based chain-link to scientifically define its inputs, outputs, or the give-gets between them. The executives had chosen to define the company's strategy based on sustainability, a differentiator. The senior sales executive stated, "Every customer that I have talked to talks about sustainability. The whole industry is being driven by sustainability." Yet, the company's chain-linked strategy map showed the give-get of sustainability with customer value and with sales was zero. Although customers talked about sustainability as a desirable feature, it had no association with customer value or sales. Increasing sustainability did not affect sales nor differentiate the company in the eyes of customers. Instead, the two biggest drivers of customer value were product quality and ongoing service and support. Senior executives centered their entire strategy planning process on sustainability due to salience. Executives failed to start with the obvious—determining what was important to customers—and then drive the strategy plan. To properly align its strategy planning, ABCO needed to flip the template it had used for decades. The company needed to start with a chain-linked strategy map, rather than a classification schematic based on convenience or tradition.

Rather than starting with a sales forecast or primary value/mission, executives must use a strategy planning template linking strategy areas to customer value. Stories from customers, employees, and other stakeholders should not drive strategy initiatives. Initiatives must be driven by areas identified as important, i.e., those with the highest give-get weights. The importance weights cannot be determined based on salient information or executives' beliefs, intuition, or gut feel. Only rigorous analysis can determine them. Executives must then use their chain-linked strategy map to drive their thinking, discussions, and decisions.

Companies are unsuccessful when senior executives start strategy planning with preconceived beliefs. When the chain-linked map becomes an add-on or "nice-to-have" feature, the strategy process is likely to be unsuccessful. It is unlikely to add value or increase financial results, even as it makes senior executives feel good.

8.6 Enabler 6: Embed Science in Strategy Planning

The vice president of research, innovation, and technology for an oilfield services company was excited about the firm's latest innovation, a drilling product sensing the external environment and adjusting speed to optimize oil output and quality. The product was created based on a precise underlying model, accurate data collected over multiple drilling runs, and data linked to the desired outcome of oil quality and quantity. The company deployed a science-based, chain-linked model to calculate the precise give-get among different inputs and outputs related to the product. The linkages between inputs, throughputs, and outputs were precisely specified so users could predict oil extraction. The R&D team used no salient information nor leaps of faith to design the drilling product. Sadly, the company did not follow the same process for strategy planning. Instead of using science, its strategy planning continued to rely on senior executives' gut feel.

A strategy planning template should not be confused with a science- and data-based model. Senior executives consistently substitute their judgment—laden with salient information, confirmation biases, and intuitive leaps—for precise, statistically derived relationships when creating strategy templates. Unlike for the drilling product, the oilfield firm's senior executives did not test their strategy model for statistical conclusion validity. In fact, the company continued to highlight the drill's environmental sustainability benefits. When asked why they focused on sustainability, executives offered no cogent response. They could not produce reliable and valid evidence to support their convictions. The reasoning proceeded as follows:

- *Salience*: Just yesterday, Shell released its sustainability report. Clearly, sustainability is critical.
- *Confirmation bias*: Most customers who have visited our R&D facility have appreciated our focus on sustainability.
- *Ignoring importance*: If we increase sustainability, customers will buy our products because they help them meet their objective. We don't have data to show increased sustainability increases customer purchase behavior, but it could not be otherwise.
- *Risk seeking due to loss aversion*: Our competitors are focused on issues like quality and safety. Through sustainability, we will differentiate ourselves. We don't have a study or data to show sustainability is a differentiator. But remember, the customers who came to our R&D center appreciated our focus on sustainability.
- *Status quo and sunk cost bias*: We have spent millions of dollars and achieved our differentiation over the last two years. Now, it is time to take it to the next level.

Executives at the company put more science in developing products and services than they put in their strategy plan. The executives, capable of using a science-based approach to create precise and complex products, created strategy without scientific measurement, an underlying chain-linked model, or data and statistical analysis. They relied mostly on hunches, gut feelings, and qualitative judgments.

Over time, the executives began using a science-based strategy template to prioritize strategy areas and initiatives based on their give-get relationship with customer value. The new template reliably predicted sales and margins. As a result, the firm's customer value increased and customers were more satisfied, even as its fixed costs and business model complexity decreased. The company began going through a systematic process to revise its strategy chain-links every 18 to 24 months using different inputs—customer surveys, financial information, costs, and operational data—subjected to machine learning models. Rather than picking and choosing based on hunches, senior executives spent more time understanding the details of their highest-ranked customer priorities. They talked to their customers to understand the nuances of their most important priorities, rather than generating the priorities based on qualitative input. The company's revamped strategy retreats started with reviewing the scientifically derived customer-value drivers and prioritizing supporting initiatives. The executives then used their chain-linked model to understand predicted sales and margins and set goals and accountability through customer, operational, and financial performance indicators. Using the science-based process provided direction to the company's strategy planning and removed bias and subjectivity. Employees began to trust the plan and feel it was believable, reliable, and useful. As the CEO stated, "Finally, the feel-good drivel is out of the strategy process, and sanity has prevailed."

8.7 Enabler 7: Approach the Planning Process with Humility

A science-based, chain-linked strategy process is most likely to succeed when senior executives—typically the CEO, CFO, and some board members—approach the endeavor with curiosity and humility. Humility does not imply an executive lacking confidence. Nor does it mean executives must accept every new idea. Rather, humility in strategy planning requires starting with the notion an executive could be wrong and his or her intuition could be less effective than a quantitative model based on data and scientific analysis. Simply acknowledging the possibility opens the door to examining assumptions and accepting science-based conclusions.

Executives with humility are able to say, "We know the strategy planning process is not working. We want to improve it using a science-based approach. We want to remain curious to learn about it and apply it." Executives lacking humility might reason, "We know the strategy process is not working. But it's not because it is broken. You have to prove it is broken. We've followed our template for so many years. Unfortunately, our market is volatile and the product commoditized."

For most executives, a lack of humility is not rooted in arrogance. Rather, it stems from fear and grooved thinking, the tendency to revert to old, familiar habits and thought patterns when faced with a lack of control or threats.[7] When individuals feel threatened, they engage in behaviors learned over time, even if the behaviors are not appropriate. They become less adaptive to the threatening situation and revert to known behaviors because they are comforting. In other words, threat-rigidity is the key reason senior executives lack humility. As the vice president of strategy at an engineering and construction company said, "I know this strategy planning approach is not working. It hasn't worked for many years. But this is what the board members want, and my job is to deliver. I've been delivering them a strategic plan for the last ten years, and they like this template." Over the next three years, as competitors' sales increased at least 30%, the engineering and construction company lost sales, market share, and margins.

8.8   Conclusion

Strategy planning enablers can be incorporated in the process at all levels. It requires senior executives and middle managers to create a strategy map, agree on the components of the map, develop their measures, rely on analysis rather than intuition and gut feel to calculate the give-get weights of each map linkage, and set aside egos, biases, and salient thoughts to accept the results of the analysis.

Although the seven strategy planning enablers presented may seem obvious to some executives, implementing them can be challenging. They require executive resolve and continuous guidance from CEOs.

Notes

1. Mason, E. Sharon, (1994), "Symbolism in managerial decision making: manipulation or inspiration?" *Journal of Managerial Psychology*, 9(6), 27–34.
2. Mintzberg, Henry (1994), "Rethinking strategic planning part I: pitfalls and fallacies," *Long Range Planning*, 27(3), 12–21.
   Lindblom, Charles E. (1959), "The science of muddling through," *Public Administration Review*, 19(2), 79–88.
3. Dawes, Robyn M. (1979), "The robust beauty of improper linear models," *American Psychologist*, 34(7), 571–582.
   Ashton, Robert (1976), "The robustness of linear models for decision-making," *Omega*, 4(5), 609–615.
4. Hall, Stephen, Dan Lovallo, and Reinier Musters (2012), "How to put your money where your strategy is," *McKinsey Quarterly*, March, 1–11.
5. Gruca, Thomas S., and Lopo L. Rego (2005), "Customer satisfaction, cash flow, and shareholder value," *Journal of Marketing*, 69(3), 115–130.

6. Mittal, Vikas, and Shrihari Sridhar (2020), "Customer based execution and strategy: Enhancing the relevance & utilization of B2B scholarship in the C-suite," *Industrial Marketing Management*, 88 (July), 396–409.
7. Staw, Barry M., Lance E. Sandelands, and Jane E. Dutton (1981), "Threat rigidity effects in organizational behavior: A multilevel analysis," *Administrative Science Quarterly*, 4(December), 501–524.

9

Exterior, Inc.'s Strategy Success Story

Senior executives can use strategy enablers to improve their company's planning and execution processes. But the executives and CEOs must internalize the enablers in their thinking and behaviors, embedding them directly within the strategy planning process. Transforming the strategy planning process requires complete commitment from senior executives and unwavering support from the CEO. Otherwise, the process inevitably retrenches into its old patterns—riddled with inhibitors, rife with conflict, and leaving goals unmet. The return to mediocrity occurs despite the best intentions of the strategy team. Everyone wants strategy to contribute to the firm's success, but the goal never materializes in the face of inhibitors.

Exterior, Inc.[1] is a strategy success story. The mid-market company's senior executives, led by their CEO, fundamentally retooled their strategy process to eliminate inhibitors and inculcate enablers. Putting aside their reliance on salient judgments, the executives embraced a science-based approach for chain-linking their strategy map and focusing their activities. How did they do it? It neither required endless training nor coaching designed to make the executives thoughtful or for browbeating them to be better leaders. The transformation happened when the firm embraced humility and recognized chain-linking the strategy process provided the answers executives needed to develop a way forward and implement it with fidelity.

© The Author(s), under exclusive license to Springer Nature Switzerland AG 2021
V. Mittal, S. Sridhar, *Focus*, https://doi.org/10.1007/978-3-030-70720-0_9

9.1   Exterior, Inc.: 2008–2014

Exterior, Inc. had built a reputation as a premium-price roof manufacturer with major product innovations to its name. Founded in 1921 with $65,000 in start-up capital, the Texas-based company began manufacturing roofing shingles to serve builders of ready-cut, or prefabricated, Midwest homes. In the first half of the twentieth century, ready-cut home builders sold houses in many different plans and styles, from simple structures to large colonials. The builders sourced and supplied all the materials needed to build houses at a fixed price for homeowners. Given Exterior's relatively high product quality, product range, and quick response times, many ready-cut home builders made the roofing company their sole supplier. To differentiate itself from competitors, Exterior invested heavily in widening its array of designs and roofing tile selection. Ultimately, it became a one-stop, exclusive supplier for several ready-cut builders.

Over time, custom-home builders emerged as a competitor for ready-cut builders. Custom-home builders offered more one-off designs, with flexible pricing based on each homeowner's selected options, and move-in ready dwellings. Exterior's offerings were even more successful with custom-home builders than ready-cut manufacturers, presumably due to the company's extensive selection, product durability, and turnkey solutions.

After a custom-home builder placed an order, Exterior shipped the material and provided a referral for a trained roofing subcontractor. Exterior built and maintained a registry of roofing installers over time. Smaller, independent custom-home builders especially valued the service, as the firms typically did not have in-house construction crews. Finding roofing subcontractors on the open market often resulted in lower margins due to increased labor costs, uneven installation quality, and delayed deliveries. Larger, corporate custom-home builders often had their own roofing crews on payroll.

By 2012, Exterior had amassed more than 150 patents, begun exporting its products to more than 50 countries, and increased the weight/thickness of its shingles to 220 pounds per square. With an industry standard of 180 pounds per square, Exterior's shingles offered increased longevity and environmental stress resistance. Exterior continued to maintain its unmatched variety of colors, textures, and aesthetics, providing three times the variety of its nearest competitor. The company's product development group took great pride in the offerings.

The 2008–2014 recession debilitated Exterior, slowing new home construction and lowering the pricing power of most custom-home builders.

Roofing manufacturers also faced stiff competition and pricing pressure at the time. Exterior's impressive 76% market share in 2007 declined to 58% by 2014. As Table 9.1 shows, gross revenue and new customer acquisitions also declined. Home construction did not return to 2004 levels until 2013, when the financial markets stabilized.

Flush with cash, new competitors from Brazil, China, and India entered the U.S. market around the time of the recession. The roofing material suppliers competed aggressively on price to gain volume and market share. In addition to lowering their prices, the foreign competitors reduced warranty lengths from ten to eight years. The companies' lower-quality products cost less to manufacture. They reasoned custom-home builders selling to first-time homeowners would trade lower prices and shorter warranties in the present against warranty-related costs eight years down the road.

9.2   Exterior's Strategy Planning Dilemma: 2014

Newly hired Exterior CEO Mike Montgomery tasked his senior executives with developing a strategy plan in 2014. His informal discussions with the team revealed Exterior suffered from many of the strategy planning frustrations described by CEOs in Chap. 2. Montgomery had inherited an internally focused strategy planning process.

The legacy strategy planning process started with the CEO, CFO, and board members setting an ambitious sales target and communicating it to other senior executives. The CFO and other executives then prepared a budget. They earmarked resources for various initiatives presented and championed by the senior executives. The team monitored the outlays throughout

Table 9.1   Exterior Inc.'s performance, 2007 versus 2014

Performance metrics	Time	
	2007	2014
Financial metrics		
Sales	$3.9 billion	$2.6 billion
EBITDA	$0.8 billion	$0.6 billion
Gross margin	22%	18%
Market share	76%	58%
Customer metrics		
New customer acquisition rate	9%	4%
Customer defection rate	12%	18%
Percentage increase in demand for 1% decrease in price	1.9%	2.1%

the year using various mechanisms—a monthly budget review meeting, quarterly budget updates, and sales reviews.

The executives hoped to meet their spending and sales growth targets each year. However, Exterior had not met its financial targets for six consecutive years. The CFO explained it was intentional. The aggressive sales target was unrealistic but designed to motivate the sales team. Other senior executives blamed the 2008–2014 economic recession.

In an initial strategy meeting, Montgomery observed Exterior's senior executives were focused on their own groups and did not fully incorporate the customer perspective in the planning process. Aside from anecdotes about customer interactions and sales figures, the new CEO saw no customer data or analysis. Each senior executive's main argument quickly boiled down to a plea for supporting initiatives and spending linked to his or her functional area. Geoffrey Prescott, vice president of sales, strongly supported a 10% price reduction. "We have lost touch with our customers and the pulse of the roofing market," he said. "It is no longer about the strongest and brightest product, but about value for money. We are at 58% market share and may lose further share if we are not priced to meet the foreign competition." According to Prescott, the sales team needed to offer an aggressive price point, and Exterior was "disillusioned about customer value."

Montgomery privately noted Prescott did not really know how much Exterior's customers valued low prices. Furthermore, did customers value low prices more or less than other factors, like product quality and variety? Montgomery suspected Prescott's assumption was driven by the salience of low prices on the minds of contractors. One such customer had just canceled an Exterior contract. Montgomery knew of several profitable and long-time clients who had never brought up price as a contentious issue during meetings. Still, it was possible both Montgomery's and Prescott's thoughts were inwardly focused and driven by salience. Neither executive knew the true importance of price in driving customer value.

Like many of the CEOs interviewed in Chap. 2, Montgomery was frustrated that meaningful and actionable information about the strategy areas driving Exterior's customers to buy was unavailable. When asked, the sales team said the information was difficult to obtain. Instead, the team presented spreadsheets comparing Exterior's prices to those of its three main competitors. The pricing charts led to several hours of discussion focused on pricing and promotion tactics. Still, no clear benchmark, data, or comparison point emerged to show how Exterior's customers felt about pricing. Not a single executive on the firm's strategy planning team could quantify the extent to which pricing drove value for custom-home builders.

Sherry McGuire, vice president of product research, was confident Exterior needed a revolutionary roofing material. She cited an industry conference she had recently attended where many competitors displayed state-of-the-art products. "We need a breakthrough product line with superior aesthetics and longer life expectancy," she said. "We are the iPhone of roofs, and let's keep it that way ... Exterior must leapfrog the competition. Our competitors are investing heavily in new product R&D, and we will lose ground unless we invest. Exterior needs to lead the industry on the product frontier, not lag."

McGuire had a doctorate in material science from Carnegie Mellon and more than 25 years' experience with manufacturing teams at Intel, 3M, and Exterior. Her knowledge about product aesthetics and life expectancy was unparalleled. She espoused a more-is-better logic. "Why wouldn't the ultimate homeowner want a better-quality roof?" she asked in one meeting. "A higher-quality roof is essential to maintaining home value. Custom-home builders know that a better-quality roof is not an expense, it's an investment." Montgomery thought McGuire's argument, like Prescott's, failed to recognize the strategy areas truly driving value for Exterior customers.

Montgomery suspected the average homebuilder did not want cutting-edge innovations every quarter. Most customers with whom Montgomery met were happy with Exterior's product quality. And more than 80% of the company's sales came from less than 25% of its catalog items. Fewer than 4% of sales came from the 15 most expensive items. Yet, Montgomery had no way of proving or disproving his gut feeling. Without a clear sense of the relative weight of product quality versus low prices, it was not obvious how executives should strategically allocate Exterior's scarce resources over the next three years.

Tamara Watkins, Exterior's chief financial officer, had different ideas. She had helped the firm's previous CEO navigate the 2008–2014 recession and believed Exterior needed a financial overhaul. "As a mid-market company, we are severely underleveraged," she said. "With interest rates at historic lows, the company needs to take on some debt and increase shareholder return. Investments in expanded product offerings can increase the Exterior brand, but with a lot of uncertainty. I haven't seen any study showing the effect of a price decrease on sales. However, simply taking on debt at this historic low interest rate will surely increase return on capital. Supplemented with aggressive cost-cutting and belt-tightening, management could create a lot of shareholder value." Montgomery thought Watkins' argument for taking on debt was logically unassailable. However, would the company lose strategy flexibility if it did so? The debt service would surely affect day-to-day cash flow.

Along with Montgomery, the senior executive team vociferously debated Prescott's, McGuire's, and Watkins' suggestions during a three-day strategy retreat. Prescott's option would sacrifice millions of dollars in margins by reducing prices to gain market share. McGuire's strategy required investing millions in R&D to improve product aesthetics and life expectancy. Everyone agreed cost-cutting was an admirable goal. However, the team could not agree on what costs to cut. The disagreements devolved into salience-based arguments and turf protection.

Montgomery's own unease about the merits of the strategy options stemmed from multiple sources. First, he was unsure if price and product quality captured the total value Exterior offered custom-home builders. What other elements might contribute to customer value? Although the company had narrowed its focus to custom-home builders, no one knew whether they were satisfying the builders' needs. Second, the strategy planning process lacked clear links showing how low prices and high product quality would improve financial outcomes. The process had become a cesspool of conflict, argumentation, and influence peddling. In the political battleground of strategy, senior executives from each camp insisted success depended on their proposed approach and blamed unsuccessful initiatives on the recession.

Montgomery had his own gut feeling. Maybe Exterior didn't need to change its prices. And perhaps the company would not have to make heavy investments in technical product attributes. What if contractors simply faced rebuy, rather than first-buy, decisions? The strategy would allow Exterior to stabilize its market share through better service. Improving the installation experience for contractors could be the key. Montgomery's solid relationship with his board gave him the confidence to override his senior executives and pursue his own strategy plan. But he hesitated to put the plan in place based on his thoughts alone. After all, the other senior executives had been with Exterior much longer than he had. He knew the executives would not give him the buy-in needed for successful implementation if they felt strategy planning was driven by CEO preferences and hunches alone. Montgomery also resisted the temptation to choose any one executive's proposed strategy based on the personal relationship or trust he shared with them. Although his relationship with Watkins was strong, he did not want to circumvent or discount the opinions of Prescott and McGuire.

Most importantly, Montgomery had the humility to accept he was no different than his senior executives. Like them, he based his strategy preferences on soft cues and gut feel. He intuited price and quality did not matter as much to customers as other factors. But the belief was laden with the same intuitive leaps and inward focus his senior executives contributed. "Fundamentally," Montgomery said to himself, "we are all just making it up as we go along. There is almost nothing but a sales forecast as the guiding star.

Even the veracity of that is dubious. We really don't have a map for our strategy. Of course, if we keep walking, we are bound to end up somewhere."

9.3 Rewiring the Strategy Planning Process: 2015

Montgomery believed fundamentally that a company's strategy goal should be to create customer value. Customers remained the largest source of cash flow for any firm. To enable Exterior's senior executives to focus their budgets, initiatives, and activities to increase customer and shareholder value, Montgomery wanted to implement a systematic, customer-focused strategy approach. He challenged his senior executives to coalesce around a chain-linked strategy map built on customer input, not subjective beliefs. "Customers are not the sideshow in the strategy plan. Customers are the show that drives revenues, cash flow, and margins," he told Prescott during a lunch meeting. "A simple or relentless focus on increasing sales is not going to put customers at the center of our strategy plan. But I do believe that sales growth can be an outcome of customer focus."

Accordingly, Montgomery asked his executives to list the elements of their strategy in an unbiased and objective manner. He then asked them to rank the elements in order of effectiveness. The exercise forced the executives to clarify and agree on strategy components, regardless of which areas they personally supported or wanted to pursue. It also enabled a free-flowing discussion about the different ways Exterior could provide value to customers. The initial discussion was broad-based and general by design. Combining their intuition from running the business for several decades and research on customer value drivers in B2B markets,[2] the executives agreed on five key strategy areas. They believed pricing, product life expectancy, product appearance, no-defect installation, and speed of installation drove value for Exterior customers. Although the team could not agree on which area most drove value, they believed improving any or all of the areas would be effective. The group engaged in several weeks of intense activity, generating industry reports and discussing Exterior's performance in the five strategy areas. McGuire commissioned a report from the product development conference she attended. The data was drawn from a study of 20 construction industry product managers. The report concluded new product development was key to differentiation. A home-builder survey showed rising material costs was a key concern among

74% of respondents. Prescott used the survey results to support his thesis that a low price was critical to gaining market share.

Montgomery realized the executives were entering another rabbit hole. The teams producing and presenting industry research on the five strategy areas unwittingly supported strategy plans pushing their own functional areas. The CEO reflected on one report emphasizing the $60 billion market potential of standing seam metal roofs. The mythical number did not relate to Exterior's customers or sales target. The intuitive leap suggesting 74% of home builders would like lower roofing prices was based on the 74% concerned about rising material costs.

After six weeks, Exterior's senior executives had cycled through more than 150 industry and macro trend reports and 15 presentations supporting each of the five strategy directions. The information failed to coalesce into a single narrative. Montgomery could see each team's report contained an implicit confirmation bias. While the executives tried to be objective, their reports were simply endorsements of the strategy areas they wanted to pursue. The team seemed to determine Exterior should pursue all five areas. Montgomery wanted to focus and sequence the company's work by determining which areas to de-prioritize and not pursue.

Montgomery also lamented that none of the reports were based on Exterior's own customers. To avoid an internally focused mindset, he asked his senior executives to develop a comprehensive and objective understanding of custom-home builders around the country. Exterior worked with an outside partner to reach out and assess custom-home builders' needs nationwide. The partner informally surveyed the builders about their needs, decision processes, and interactions with Exterior and its competitors. The partner then used Exterior's custom-home builder database to conduct a statistically representative customer assessment. In 2015, the outside partner sent the assessment to 1200 custom-home builders across the United States. Among them, 486 builders completed the survey, with 85% of the respondents being small builders completing fewer than five projects per year.

The assessment measured customer value in the five strategy areas: pricing, product life expectancy, product looks, no-defect installation, and speed of installation. It also obtained measures of the overall value customers received from Exterior, their likelihood to use the firm for their next job, and whether they would recommend Exterior to colleagues. The company's performance as perceived by its customers and measured on a 0–100 scale is shown in Table 9.2. The external partner provided benchmark averages from a select group of competitors rated by the same customers. The competitor

Table 9.2   Customer assessment results, 2015

Strategic area	Exterior's performance	Competitor performance
Pricing	80	82
Product life expectancy	79	81
No-defect installation	74	82
Speed of installation	73	82
Product looks (aesthetics)	64	77
Overall customer value	73	81

Source: Four hundred eighty-six assessments of roofing contractors

information allowed Exterior to gauge its relative performance. It performed poorly relative to competitors in all five strategy areas.

As Table 9.2 shows, Exterior's performance ranged from 64 to 80 in the five strategy areas. Its poorest relative performance was in product looks (64). Its best performance (80) was in pricing. Overall, Exterior provided low customer value. Its overall value score of 73 was lower than its competitors' average of 81. The stark performance gap between customer value as perceived by Exterior's customers and the B2B industry average was a watershed moment in the company's strategy journey.

Montgomery and other senior executives had been frustrated the information they used for strategy planning was fragmented and provided no context. Understanding Exterior's own customers and competitors helped the executives agree the company was not performing as well as they thought. Montgomery suspected the company's mediocre performance was the result of attempts to force initiatives related to all five strategy elements into the strategy plan. The result was a decade-long diffuse focus. While trying to be excellent in all five strategy areas, Exterior failed to be even average in any area.

Exterior's outside partner showed Montgomery and his team that B2B companies could gain between 8% and 12% in revenue by bridging a nine-point gap in customer value. Linking the results to Exterior's customer base and sales, the partner created an empirical model showing a nine-point customer value increase at Exterior translated to $208 million to $312 million of incremental revenue.[3] The benefit of increasing customer value provided Montgomery and his executive team clarity and focus. They understood why and how they should coalesce around customer value. No longer did the team need mythical numbers or intuitive leaps to set Exterior's strategy plan. Along with CFO Watkins, Montgomery met with his board to state the company's goal of growing sales by 11% in three years. He told board members Exterior's strategy was to grow sales by increasing customer value and bridging the nine-point gap with competitors. In doing so, Montgomery and his team took responsibility for Exterior's strategy and sales growth goal, and they stopped making excuses for past performance. The CEO laid out his vision for aligning his senior executives and delivering a strategy implementation plan that would focus and sequence their activities.

Implementing the strategy required carefully deciding the areas where the senior executives should focus their attention and sequence their work. Strategy planning fosters a tendency to do more—more projects, more initiatives—to improve performance. The CEOs interviewed in Chap. 2, for example, lamented the tendency of senior executives to believe everything is important and add initiatives.

On which of the five areas should Exterior's senior executives focus over 18 months to close the nine-point customer value gap and achieve sales growth? The company performed poorly on all five areas. McGuire, the product research director, suggested product longevity and aesthetics. "The low customer value for product looks clearly shows the need to refresh the product line," she said. "Only by investing in product can we increase customer value." Prescott offered similar arguments for his own functional area, stating the urgent need to "double down on pricing, the best performing area according to our customers." Montgomery was unconvinced. Exterior still didn't know which of the strategy areas were most important to its customers.

Because customers were not as satisfied with Exterior's product appearance, the strategy area was salient to senior executives. The same argument could be made for the other four areas. They were salient to executives because of poor performance. But how important were they really to Exterior's customers? If Montgomery could rank the strategy areas based on their importance in driving customer value and sales, Exterior could focus its attention on the most critical areas and de-emphasize less critical areas.

Quantifying the give-get of each linkage between inputs and outputs in a firm's strategy map is critical to ordering priorities. Exterior's executives wanted to build their strategy around the strongest linkages between strategy areas and financial performance measures, not the weakest linkages. They again turned to the external partner to quantify the relative importance of each strategy area in determining customer value. As shown in Table 9.3, product life expectancy had the lowest importance weight at 3%. Next was product looks at 12%. Speed of installation (40%), no-defect installation (27%), and pricing (18%): each was important. Subsequent conversations with customers revealed they did not want the lowest price. Rather, they wanted a fair price and a way to find reliable roofing installers quickly.

Table 9.3 helped Exterior's executives put aside their salient beliefs and rely on what was important to their customers. They could see 67% of their customer value came from the installation process, with 40% coming from speed

Table 9.3 Customer assessment results, 2015

Strategic area	Exterior's performance	Competitor average	Strategic area importance
Pricing	80	82	18
Product life expectancy	79	81	3
No-defect installation	74	82	27
Speed of installation	73	82	40
Product looks	64	77	12
Overall customer value	73	81	

Source: Four hundred eighty-six assessments of roofing contractors

and 27% from no defects. They knew Exterior performed poorly on both areas compared to competitors. The company lagged by nine points on installation speed and eight points on no-defect installation. If Exterior wanted to grow revenue by $208 million to $312 million, Montgomery said the company should focus all its resources and initiatives on installation. Product aesthetics and pricing provided only one-third of all customer value. By trying to excel in the areas unimportant to customers, executives would remain distracted. Montgomery emphasized Exterior should treat pricing and aesthetics as strategy areas of sufficiency and resist the urge to add initiatives in those areas. Because the focus was based on statistically determined customer value instead of intuitive leaps or salience, the senior executives found it easy to rally behind the new approach. Montgomery had gained his senior executives' commitment to the strategy plan by putting customers at the center.

9.4 Exterior's Strategy Enabled Not Inhibited: 2015–2017

Once Exterior's executives agreed price and product aesthetics would be areas of sufficiency and installation speed and no-defect installation would be areas of excellence, the company gained focus and clarity. Previously, though, senior executives had not focused their attention on the installation process, and they had a lot to learn.

The four senior executives—Montgomery, Prescott, McGuire, and Watkins—met with Exterior's distributors, key clients, roofing installers, and frontline employees. They wanted to truly understand the product installation process. They learned Exterior's entire distribution chain, from manufacturing to distribution to installation, was fragmented and disconnected. The sales department did not have a robust list of the custom-home builders using Exterior's products, whether the roofs were installed on time, or if there were errors during installation. Exterior's distributors did not maintain clean time sheets on installation. And although the company shipped material directly to building sites and home builders, the users did not maintain records with sufficient integrity. As a consequence, no one at Exterior could answer two simple questions: (1) How long does it take for a custom-home builder to receive roofing material after placing an order? and (2) What percentage of installations are without defects?

Exterior's senior executives were able to obtain data on recorded installation accidents when insurance claims were filed by custom-home builders or distributors. The users filed claims for egregious blunders during installation, but the Exterior executives also had to sift through many disparate records of errors by certified installers. Rumors among distributors suggested Exterior never bothered to check in with custom-home builders after the firm shipped material. "These claims are only the tip of the iceberg," McGuire said. "The rate of errors in the installation process has got to be much higher."

Over several weeks, the Exterior executives met regularly to improve their collective understanding of the installation process. They looked for ways to improve installation, achieve buy-in from middle management and frontline employees, and develop a plan of action. "Installation excellence is now our calling card," Montgomery said. "This is what our customers value, and here is where we will excel."

In October 2015, Montgomery and his three top executives announced a partnership with Exterior's major distributors, rolling out a mix of technology and teamwork to "ensure that all custom-home builders would obtain a no-defect shingle within 10 business days of ordering, along with referrals to at least three roofing subcontractors trained by Exterior." Prior to the partnership, the executives discussed the goals with several large and small custom-home builders. The feedback was universally positive. Anything improving installation process timeliness or reducing the pain of mistakes would be a huge differentiator. "Now that I carefully think about it, a good install is more important than a price discount or a product variation," one home builder said.

The approach incorporated two strategy planning enablers, "Achieve More by Doing Less" and "Chain-link Your Strategy Map," outlined in Chap. 8. Achieving more by doing less during strategy implementation requires embracing a system-wide data collection effort. The effort must encompass all key initiatives and projects and analyze them using advanced statistical models to link inputs, throughputs, and outputs. Exterior used the process to arrive at the performance indicators truly reflecting customer value from the home builder's perspective. The firm then linked the indicators to a set of internally tracked operational metrics and used the linkages to develop a financial model for sales prediction. Rather than tracking a large number of metrics bifurcated from reality, causing analysis paralysis, and failing to focus and sequence executives' work, Exterior focused on one strategy area of excellence.

The company made several investments and began measuring its progress on installation initiatives. Prescott led the tracking system's development. Specifically, the system did the following:

- Started to track the average number of days required to deliver each batch of roofing material to a distributor's warehouse.
- Invested in developing a national, searchable database linked to an automated system that

  - referred custom-home builders to the three physically closest certified roofing subcontractors within two business days of confirming the builder's order;
  - followed up with custom-home builders by phone to verify their chosen roofing subcontractor within 48 hours; and
  - connected distributors and roofing subcontractors to ensure distributors delivered materials to home locations by subcontractors' chosen dates.

- Measured distributors on the number of days required to deliver products to roofing subcontractors and put the ratings in a national database.
- Rated roofing subcontractors on the number of days required to finalize installation and obtain a no-defect signature from custom-home builders.

Through its outside partner, Exterior also measured the value custom-home builders' derived from the installation being completed within four weeks. Exterior hired 50 service-support managers distributed throughout the United States to help gather, process, and share feedback on delivery speed, installation speed, and installation quality. McGuire led the initiative. For each job, Exterior collected metrics on the speed and quality of work performed and updated its roofing subcontractor referral database. The firm also developed and sponsored a two-day training session for distributors to share delivery and installation best practices. The seminar sought to standardize and systematize success stories from top-performing distributors.

Effective strategy implementation requires senior executives, middle management, and frontline employees to work on a few—but highly important—inputs driving customer value and, eventually, sales. But strategy planning often suffers from a paradox. While many senior executives are able to deploy more resources to prioritized areas, they are rarely successful at de-emphasizing low-priority areas. To tackle the strategy planning inhibitor, Montgomery and his three senior executives committed to creating a not-to-do list while pursuing excellence in the installation process. The not-to-do list included several significant efforts:

- Prescott led an effort requiring all sales personnel to offer no price reductions or matches for 18 months. If sales leaders needed an exception, they would draft a one-page memo to Prescott offering their reasoning. Prescott, Montgomery, and Watkins reviewed each request before approving a price reduction. They received 89 requests from 2015 to 2017 and approved only one price reduction, making it clear lowering prices was not a strategy lever for Exterior. Jointly reviewing each request, though time consuming, provided the CEO, CFO, and senior sales executive with a deep understanding of the sales process.
- McGuire led an effort to defund all R&D projects focused on product variety from 2016 onward. She spearheaded a new set of projects to reduce installation times for existing products by 10% or decrease installation defects.
- Exterior hired a branding agency for its marketing communications in the trade press, at trade shows, in public relations, for online advertising, and on its website. Exterior previously emphasized a generic brand position: "Improving homes, improving lives." Under guidance from Prescott and McGuire, the company revamped its messaging to emphasize its installation advantages. All of Exterior's customer-facing communications focused on the ways defect-free and faster installation improved value for home builders and homeowners.

The simultaneous increased emphasis on a single strategy area of excellence and decreased emphasis on strategy areas of sufficiency began to pay off by 2017. In June that year, Exterior conducted a follow-up customer assessment to measure its progress. The results are shown in Table 9.4.

Exterior's overall customer value increased from 73 in 2015 to 84 in 2017. The firm accomplished its goal of increasing customer value by nine points and then some. The senior executives were elated but not surprised to find Exterior's improvement came from their new strategy areas of excellence.

Table 9.4   Customer assessment results, 2017

Strategic area	Exterior's performance (2015)	Exterior's performance (2017)
Pricing	80	81
Product life expectancy	79	80
No-defect installation	74	88
Speed of installation	73	89
Product looks (aesthetics)	64	68
Overall customer value	73	84

Source: Four hundred eighty-six assessments of roofing contractors

No-defect installation improved from 74 to 88, and installation speed improved from 73 to 89. On the strategy areas of sufficiency—pricing, product looks, and product life expectancy—Exterior's performance remained at 2015 levels. The strategy transformation translated to increased customer value, a 11% sales increase, and a 13% increase in new customer acquisitions. By cutting costs in areas customers did not value, Exterior also lowered its fixed costs and increased margins by 0.5%. "Finally, Exterior has attained a distinct competitive advantage," Watkins said. "The system we have put in place to excel in installation cannot be easily replicated by any competitor, and we don't have to compete on price anymore. What more can a CFO ask?"

Heading into 2020, Exterior's senior executives continued to focus on the installation process. They clearly communicated the strategy area of excellence to middle management, frontline employees, and customers. Critical suppliers, such as roofing installers and distributors, fully understood installation excellence was the bedrock of Exterior's strategy. The transformation Montgomery put in place to eliminate strategy inhibitors and inculcate enablers empowered his team and rewarded personnel for industry-leading service.

9.5   Conclusion

Many CEOs are frustrated with their company's strategy process. Chapter 7 documents the seven primary strategy inhibitors fueling the chief executives' frustration. Chapter 8 shows how seven enablers can improve the strategy planning process.

As Exterior's journey demonstrates, transforming an existing strategy planning process to replace the inhibitors with enablers requires deep CEO commitment. The transformation requires more than general attempts to coach senior executives on decision-making skills, teamwork, and leadership. It requires the executives to have a deep level of trust and humility to forego their salience-based notions of strategy planning and how the process can be transformed through scientific approaches like chain-linking inputs and outputs. As Montgomery, McGuire, Prescott, and Watkins demonstrated, it requires close collaboration among senior executives and a willingness to internalize the enablers in the day-to-day grind of developing the planning process and designing and implementing a strategy.

Exterior is one company where all the enablers coalesced to bring customers into the strategy planning and implementation process. And the firm completed the transformation in the face of inhibitors consistently threatening to turn back the clock on its updated process.

Notes

1. The name and key features of the company and its executives have been altered to maintain anonymity.
2. Mittal, Vikas, and Shrihari Sridhar (2020), "Customer-based strategy and execution in business-to-business firms: Enhancing the relevance & utilization of B2B scholarship in the C-suite," *Industrial Marketing Management*, 88(July), 396–409.
3. Best, Roger, Vikas Mittal, and Shrihari Sridhar (2021), *Market-Based Management*, 7th edition (forthcoming).

10

Increasing the Strategy Planning Quotient

A senior private equity firm partner who routinely hires CEOs for the group's companies said chief executives and other senior executives add value to a company in many ways. "The right senior executive can make or break the company," the senior partner said. The partner further explained his group "hired senior executives for many different purposes."

Companies may hire one of at least four senior executive types, depending on their goals:

Firefighter-in-chief. Firefighters-in-chief add value by turning specific situations around. For example, one owner suffered health issues immediately after the company was acquired by a private equity group. The group brought in a CEO to smooth the transition and stabilize the acquired firm. After six months, the firefighter-in-chief helped the private equity group hire a new, long-term CEO.

Implementer-in-chief. An implementer-in-chief performs key tasks with competence and fidelity with minimal supervision. The executive's main goal is to manage a company objective through completion. For example, one private equity fund retains a chief technology officer whose job is to review and fix the IT infrastructure of every acquired company within nine months. The fund sometimes hires a chief HR officer whose primary role is to release underperforming employees and ensure each performance evaluation system is compliant with basic employment regulations.

Counselor-in-chief. Some CEOs and senior executives are hired to develop and mentor younger or inexperienced team members. Inventors and entrepreneurs launching companies often need mentorship to mature as executives.

V. Mittal, S. Sridhar, *Focus*, https://doi.org/10.1007/978-3-030-70720-0_10

Counselors-in-chief act as executive coaches, help manage and smooth interpersonal relationships among executives, build executive teams through hiring, empower others to act, and build engagement and teamwork.

Strategy-leader-in-chief. The strategy-leader-in-chief adds value by enabling senior executives to develop a focused and sequenced strategy. The executive prioritizes company initiatives and allows others to prioritize their time and work. The strategy leading CEO uses the HR group to act as counselors, taps the COO to implement specific projects and initiatives, and enables other senior executives to firefight when needed. The main contribution of the executive, though, remains developing and executing a strategy plan to deliver shareholder value.

10.1   Not All CEOs Are Strategy Leaders

The board member of one mid-market company said a strategy-leader-in-chief is a special CEO. "The strategy leading CEO has the humility to understand and accept cause-and-effect relationships that violate preconceived notions, is self-aware, and has the ability to guide other executives to make decisions that are based on data and not gut feel," the board member said.

The CEO of Exterior, Inc. exhibited the qualities of a strategy-leading chief executive. He did not jump into firefighting to combat foreign competitors entering the roofing market. Nor did he wade into the weeds of implementation, trying to micromanage Exterior's pricing strategy or R&D portfolio. He resisted the temptation to play counselor-in-chief and build bridges among his senior executives. Any one of the temptations had the potential to derail Exterior's strategy and turn the planning process into a sideshow.

Exterior's CEO enabled his senior executives through a strategy planning process that focused their work on areas driving customer value and improving sales and margins. Using the strategy planning enablers described in Chap. 8, the CEO employed external resources to root out salience, reduce reliance on gut feel, and focus on strategy inputs with the highest weight in determining relevant outcomes. He led with humility. Rather than forcing his point of view on others, he helped his senior executives overcome salience-based biases, eliminated intuitive leaps, and developed a strategy map. The approach minimized politics, lobbying, and conflict among Exterior's senior executives. They critically examined the firm's strategy planning and implementation. Most of their conversations moved away from "what feels right" or "what my experience tells me" to "what are the important inputs on which we need to focus to drive customer value and eventually sales and margins?"

Each of the eight companies described in Chap. 1 had unique executives. Some were counselors, some were firefighters, some were implementers. A few were strategy leaders:

EPCO's CEO as counselor-in-chief. As EPCO's sales declined, its CEO employed team building activities to bring the firm's project management and sales groups together. The CEO asked EPCO's CFO to counsel the senior sales executive after putting resources into the sales and bidding group. Eventually, the chief executive replaced the CFO, senior vice president of sales, and vice president of projects, hoping new personnel could turn the company around. Yet, hampered by an inward focus, no turnaround occurred. The company's bid-win rate of 28% dropped even further the next year. After another dismal year due to more cancelled projects and rising fixed costs, the CEO left the company.

FOODCO's CEO as firefighter-in-chief. In the face of the FOODCO owner's strong personality, the group's CEO simply stopped engaging in strategy. Over time, the executive took on the role of lead firefighter, tackling issues the owner identified. On any given day, the CEO might fulfill the responsibilities of project manager or frontline employee. Operating with a firefighter-in-chief, FOODCO was not able to increase sales or gain market share. It continued as a family-owned business with an ineffective CEO who had endeared himself to the company owner. "He listens well and is easy to work with," the owner said.

TOOLCO's project management president as implementer- and counselor-in-chief. Rather than conducting strategy and explaining the group's contribution to the CEO, the TOOLCO project management president simply managed projects in the division. The executive focused on ensuring a cordial relationship with vice presidents and directors and making them feel empowered. TOOLCO's elaborate strategy retreat was participative and democratic. The project management president's direct reports laid out the group's agenda and decided on the projects to pursue. Although the group president was instrumental in putting in place a 360-degree customer relationship management (CRM) system and designed quality control training modules, the group struggled to be seen as a strategy asset, rather than an expense.

SCHOOLCO's CEO as firefighter-in-chief. Without a clear strategy and focus on initiatives, the SCHOOLCO CEO fought fires on a day-to-day basis. The organization's board members laid out specific initiatives they believed would benefit students and viewed the CEO as a caretaker. With the chief executive's contract renewed, not much changed for SCHOOLCO. Halfway through the CEO's new term, the district was unable to discontinue a single initiative, despite school enrolment declining for almost five years.

REALTYCO's and MEDCO's CEOs as implementers-in-chief. The REALTYCO and MEDCO CEOs continued to implement a sales strategy to increase clientele, build social media presence, and integrate technology. At REALTYCO, major projects implemented include upgrading property management software and using spreadsheets to manage weekly work orders for repairs. MEDCO's CEO continued on the same track, as well. With its medical software upgraded, the group began providing online visits during the COVID-19 pandemic.

FACILITYCO'S CEO as strategy-leader-in-chief. To resist becoming an implementer-in-chief, FACILITYCO's CEO hired a senior vice president of strategy to uproot the firm's existing strategy planning process, eliminate salience-based decisions, and develop a chain-linked strategy map. The new strategy officer collaborated with an external partner to conduct a comprehensive assessment of clients, employees, and senior executives. Based on the client assessment, the executive identified two strategy areas that added the most value to FACILITYCO customers, chain-linked them to sales growth, and focused the company's efforts on delivering error-free service. The firm's senior executives, guided by the CEO, reduced its strategy initiatives from 21 to 8. After less than one year, FACILITYCO achieved its short-term sales and margin goals. After less than two years, the company had gained market share from major competitors and increased customer value.

ABCO's CEO as strategy-leader-in-chief. Starting with a blank slate, ABCO's CEO set out to develop a customer-focused strategy. The CEO tasked the firm's chief revenue officer and chief financial officer to analyze the factors driving value for its customers. The chief executive partnered with an external group and determined on-time delivery and communication-effectiveness were the company's main customer value drivers. In addition, the group used statistical analysis to link customer value to sales and developed a sales projection. The ABCO CEO then began guiding senior executives to implement a chain-linked strategy, rather than relying on intuitive leaps and salience. Prior to developing the strategy map, ABCO's 12 senior executives were misaligned on the factors driving customer value. They became 100% aligned behind improving on-time delivery and communication-effectiveness.

The CEOs at Exterior, FACILITYCO, and ABCO show how senior executives can replace strategy inhibitors with enablers, and resolve the strategy planning frustrations experienced by so many companies. Over time, CEOs, senior executives, and their firms can improve their strategy planning quotient with simple but powerful changes.

10.2 How Can CEOs Increase Their Strategy Planning Quotient?

CEOs can dramatically improve their strategy planning quotient and the value they bring to the planning process by following a few simple guidelines:

- *Understand the differences among CEO types.* An understanding of CEO types can allow you to make a conscious transformation from a firefighting, implementing, or counseling CEO to a strategy-leading CEO. Discuss the transformation plan with your board and apprise them of the approach you intend to take.
- *Quantify the linkage between customer value and sales growth, and make sure your executives internalize it.* If you communicate one thing repeatedly to senior executives, make it this: do not underestimate the financial benefits of improving customer value. Most senior executives become inwardly focused because they make this mistake. By quantifying how customer value can predict sales growth and margins, CEOs ensure employees and other senior executives remain externally focused.
- *Replace the salience-based strategy process with a chain-linked strategy.* The transformation requires a blunt and objective commitment to yourself:

  - Meet frequently with your direct reports to decide on strategy inputs and outputs. If necessary, visualize your strategy map, agree on how it will be measured, and statistically quantify the give-get of each input, throughput, and output linkage. For example, Exterior executives all agreed on the goal of improving sales and margins through customer value. They agreed the give-get for customer value was stronger for installation than for price or product quality. The decision was not made through gut feeling or argument, but through a statistically valid approach.
  - Ensure your senior executives use relative strategy area importance, not personal salience, to make decisions. Demonstrate a culture of humility

in which you are willing to accept recommendations from your formal strategy map. Only by your example will senior executives become comfortable accepting the statistically derived input rankings and giving up salience-based decision-making.

- Discourage using personal preferences as strategy drivers. Making executives drop personal biases is one of the biggest challenges and contributions of strategy-leading CEOs.
- Empower senior executives to develop solutions for the eight CEO frustrations outlined in Chap. 2.
- Hold your senior executives firmly accountable for their no-to-do lists. Use phrases like "let's defer it for another three quarters," "not never but not now," and "focus on completing X during Q1 and then Y in Q2." As a strategy-leading CEO, your primary contribution is reducing each senior executive's scope of work.
- Infuse the strategy process with analytics specific to your company. Broad-based industry, sector, and global trends might inform your industry knowledge, but they lack the specificity and relevance needed to serve as the basis for your strategy.
- Remind your senior executives companies spend hundreds of thousands—if not millions—of dollars analyzing downstream decisions in product development, budgeting, and pricing. They have leagues of analysts determining the precise relationship between things like automobile metal thickness and safety. Yet, the same companies rely on gut feel to create strategy and drive the daily jobs of thousands of employees. CEOs are in the best position to break the cycle.

• *Treat strategy planning and implementation as the central contribution you and your senior executives make to your company.* Most senior executives spend most of their time managing politics and firefighting. Less than 20% of their time is spent on strategy planning or understanding customers. Make time in your calendar to work through your strategy plan to protect yourself from daily emergencies, project management, and counselling.

• *Avoid analysis paralysis and rabbit holes.* A statistically valid strategy map allows you to rank customer needs, decide specific execution levers, and prioritize initiatives based on their sales impact. If your executives go down rabbit holes or say things like, "because I don't understand it, it must be wrong" or "unless you can explain it to me, we should stop everything," you need to intervene.

- *Be tough and follow your strategy plan with complete fidelity.* As the strategy process unfolds, some senior executives will be unwilling to give up their old ways. Be firm and make the tough calls—even the really tough calls.

10.3 How Can Senior Executives Increase Their Strategy Planning Quotient?

Although crucial to strategy planning's success, senior executives play a different role than CEOs. The CEO must make the decision to adopt a specific strategy planning approach. While senior executives can nudge and push, they must not take it upon themselves to change their CEO's approach.

Once CEOs are open to improving their own strategy planning quotient, senior executives can contribute in many ways. Exterior's successful strategy planning process transformation and improved financial outcomes cannot be attributed to CEO Mike Montgomery alone. The company's three senior executives contributed by improving their own strategy planning quotient and embracing a new paradigm. Similarly, FACILITYCO's senior vice president of strategy played a transformative role by developing a strategy map that infused customer value into everything the firm did. The senior executive led the effort to link customer value to sales, helping the CEO develop an internal communication plan. At ABCO, the CEO relied heavily on the CFO and chief revenue officer to educate the remaining nine senior executives on the company's new strategy approach.

Senior executives can increase their strategy planning quotient and help their CEO and company improve by adhering to a few simple precepts:

1. *Learn and understand your CEO's type.* If your CEO is not a strategy leader, orient the chief executive to the benefits of strategy. However, realize it is neither your job nor your responsibility to make the CEO focus on strategy. When senior executives try to change or "manage" their CEO to achieve a certain outcome, the effort tends to end poorly.
2. *Recognize your inhibitors and replace them with enablers.* For a typical senior executive, the biggest inhibitor is the salience of past experience. Simply because you've done something a certain way for a long time, you believe you should continue doing so. At ABCO, the vice president of sales said, "we are terrible at after-sales service, because only yesterday a major client was complaining. We need to add more service reps to increase sales." The argument was salience-based. When the CFO pointed out that no

correlation existed between the number of service representatives and customer complaints or sales, the sales executive had the humility to admit his point of view was based on salience, rather than after-sales service importance.

3. *Tame strategy inhibitors by adopting science-based models and continuous practice.* Senior executives tend to make intuitive leaps, use mythical numbers, and overemphasize salient incidents. The errors occur when the executives use reports about macro-trends to push initiatives and ignore the initiatives' statistical importance, as shown in a chain-linked strategy map specific to their company. Through continuous and deliberative practice, train yourself to use customer-based models and make your company externally focused.

4. *Recognize and appreciate the impact and power of customer value for predicting financial performance.* CFOs can use the statistical association between customer value and company performance for more accurate sales forecasts and financial planning. A senior vice president of sales might use it to plan the sales process and win more bids. COOs can use the association to streamline initiatives that contribute most to customer value. Many senior executives hamper their CEO's work and leave money on the table by underestimating the benefits of increased customer value. The error leaves middle management and frontline employees disheartened because they do not understand why they must focus on customer value.

5. *Develop your functional group's not-to-do list.* By syncing your group's not-to-do list with the company's, you can assist the CEO in streamlining resource allocation and focusing the firm in one direction. At ABCO, 12 senior executives enabled their CEO and chief revenue officer to streamline initiatives and eliminate 23 out of 34 ongoing programs.

6. *Change your strategy mindset from abstract to science-based.* By carefully defining strategy inputs and outputs, measuring them with precision, and using high-level statistical techniques to chain-link them, you can bring strategy planning out of the dark ages. Companies use a science-based approach to optimize workflows, design manufacturing plants, and develop products. Why leave strategy to chance when you can make it repeatable and objective and enhance the value you bring to your company?

When a company's senior executives and CEO decide to increase their strategy planning quotient, they'll reap even more benefits from upgrading their strategy process. The process in most companies is ossified, a variation of something done for many years. The strategy process for the companies is essentially a planning cycle used to determine short- or medium-term objectives and allocate budget. As described by the CEOs interviewed in Chap. 2, most strategy planning processes are inward looking and do not accomplish the core objective of differentiating the firm based on customer value and improving its long-term sales potential.

10.4 Review and Refine Your Company's Strategy Process

The top employees in any company—the CEO's direct and indirect reports—should take the strategy planning quotient quiz in Chap. 1. How do they score on average? A relatively low score (below 80) might be a concern. If some score high and others low, senior executives may suffer from disagreement and dispersion.

All CEOs and senior executives should review their strategy planning process regularly. Start the review by objectively answering a few key questions:

a. What strategy planning approach—budget-based, mission-vision based, or adhocratic—does your company use? Likely, you use a mix of all three. Senior executives like to talk about mission, vision, and values but also frequently engage in sales planning and budgeting.
b. Do you use a formal (i.e., statistical) process for linking metrics to each other and to sales and margins?
c. Does your strategy plan measure customer value and link it to financial outcomes?
d. In the past ten years, how many times has your company met its sales goal? When you missed the goal, could you statistically link the issue to specific actions?
e. Does your company confuse strategy planning with project and sales planning?

An honest strategy planning diagnosis is a significant first step in fixing the process. Start with a simple visual of a chain-linked strategy map with no numbers or data. The CEO of ABCO and senior strategy executive at FACILITYCO started with a model drawn on a sheet of paper. The executives refined the model through discussions and came to agreement about inputs and outputs and their measures. They developed comfort with the external partner measuring their key performance indicators (KPIs), the statistical analysis chain-linking their strategy, and interpreting the strategy map. The process required close collaboration among executives and the humility to accept a new and objective strategy development approach.

Remember the following when reviewing and refining your company's strategy planning process:

Evaluate whether your company has a systematic approach to measuring and chain-linking KPIs. Most companies do not have a systematic approach to KPIs. To improve your company's strategy process, executives must organize and link a small set of metrics. Rather than measuring and managing many KPIs, find a few falling in one of three categories:

- *Customer KPIs measuring value and company performance from the customer's perspective.* Customer KPIs can be based on surveys, measured behaviors, or outcomes like sales.
- *Operational KPIs measuring employee-specific activities, processes, and internal outcomes.* Operational KPIs can include activity rates and measures, supply-chain metrics, and HR and accounting metrics, among others.
- *Financial KPIs measuring monetary outcomes.* Financial KPIs typically include sales, revenues, margins, profits, ROI/ROA, and other down-stream metrics.

By measuring only financial KPIs, executives provide weak and insufficient direction to senior executives and frontline employees. Operational and customer KPIs can provide specific and timely feedback.[1] At ABCO, the most important KPIs included customer value (measured as satisfaction), the percentage of customers asking ABCO for a quote, and the percentage of submitted quotes won. Statistical analysis showed a strong association among customer value, bid invitation, and bid winning. The demonstrable association helped ABCO's CEO and senior executives devise a reality-based strategy plan. The company then linked customer value to the operational KPIs of on-time delivery and communication-effectiveness. It tracked the number of days from ordering to final delivery and hours required to return service requests. Focusing on fewer than five operational KPIs simplified executives' work and activities.

Determine if the strategy process correctly distinguishes customer value from sales and sales from margins. Customer value drives sales. Yet, increased sales do not necessarily drive margins. The relationships differ for every company. To put in place a robust strategy process, the relationships must be determined at the customer, branch, or transaction level. Although initiatives may be spear-headed by different executives, they must not devolve into functional silos. Functional excellence alone does not contribute to customer value, increased sales, or strategy success. A planning process relating every strategy area to a functional area is less likely to be successful than a process encouraging executives to collaborate.

Eschew broad-based trends at the sector, industry, economy, or macro level as the basis of strategy. Broad-based trends mostly encourage intuitive leaps, use of mythical numbers, and salience-based strategy approaches. They cannot be credibly linked to an individual company's performance. Instead, they turn strategy into a look-alike clone of the many companies comprising the trends.

Remember to communicate. Senior executives must ensure employees understand the basis of their company's chain-linked strategy. Executives must also listen to employees, suppliers, and other stakeholders to ensure their interests are aligned with customers. Proper alignment requires understanding the give-get of various strategy map inputs.

10.5 Creating a Robust Strategy Planning Framework

Discussions with CEOs shows five repeatable and predictable milestones occur in most companies' strategy planning journey.[2] The milestones (see Fig. 10.1) can help a company structure its strategy plan in a repeatable, measurable, and concrete way.

Milestone 1: Setting financial goals and targets based on customer value. CEOs hold themselves accountable to their boards and shareholders by setting measurable financial goals. They can enhance the strategy planning process by basing their financial goals on customer value rather than guesswork and gut feel. By clearly quantifying the association between customer value and financial outcomes, CEOs can peg financial targets to how well their company satisfies its customers. The outcome of the strategy planning stage should include an integrated set of financial metrics. The metrics should provide a measure of the company's current and future health. Benchmarking the metrics—sales and customer value—on a consistent basis enables CEOs to hold themselves and their senior executives accountable. Systematically measuring customer value and corresponding financial metrics and relating the metrics statistically isolates the confounding effect of external factors.

Milestone 2: Prioritizing strategy areas that support financial targets and identifying execution levers. Basing financial targets on customer value enables CEOs to provide senior executives with a credible blueprint for chain-linking strategy. Senior executives can work together to determine the strategy areas and corresponding priorities that best deliver customer value and support the

Milestone 5: Measuring and benchmarking results

Milestone 1: Setting financial goals and targets based on customer value

Milestone 4: Tracking implementation through a small set of predictive KPIs

Milestone 2: Prioritizing strategic areas supporting the financial targets and identifying execution levers

Milestone 3: Focusing and sequencing initiatives and activities

Fig. 10.1 Strategy process milestones

CEO's financial targets. The best way to determine and organize the priorities is by using their impact on customer value. Most executives agree their business primarily exists to satisfy customers. At Exterior, senior executives prioritized no-defect and timely installation as strategy areas supporting customer value. Defining and prioritizing strategy areas should not be done using salience. The process must be based on a rigorous customer-needs analysis and assigning each need an appropriate weight.

Milestone 3: Focusing and sequencing initiatives and activities. CEOs must channel their senior executives' time and energy into a small set of meaningful activities. Once the executives agree on the strategy areas driving customer value, they can also agree on a small set of initiatives corresponding to the areas. At Exterior, the senior executives agreed installation would be their focal strategy area before developing initiatives to improve their installation processes. Senior executives can then rally their direct reports—directors and senior managers—to implement their firm's chosen initiatives. Linking specific initiatives to strategy areas and critical execution levers helps all personnel focus and sequence their activities. Rather than engaging in any and every initiative or activity, middle managers and frontline employees can channel their work on the initiatives directly supporting the most important strategy areas. Strategy areas of excellence have the highest weight in driving customer value, while areas of sufficiency have low or no weight. For Exterior, installation became the strategy area of excellence. Pricing and product quality became strategy areas of sufficiency.

Milestone 4: Tracking implementation through a small set of predictive KPIs. The fourth milestone of the B2B strategy journey focuses on tracking implementation through KPIs in strategy areas of excellence. Exterior used customer and operational KPIs statistically linked to two strategy areas of excellence, timely delivery and error-free installation. Frontline employees, their supervisors, and line managers are in direct contact with customers and accountable for conducting activities directly affecting relevant outcomes. By providing them with a small set of KPIs, senior executives can give employees clarity in satisfying the most important customer needs.

Milestone 5: Measuring and benchmarking results. Ongoing strategy implementation requires measuring and benchmarking at all company levels. The CEO must report results to the board. Senior executives report results to the CEO. Middle management reports to senior executives. And frontline employees report to middle management. Measuring results requires isolating a small set of customer, operational, and financial KPIs predicting customer value and sales growth. The CEO, senior executives, and middle managers must statistically measure whether their initiatives and activities, designed to drive customer value and financial performance, improve KPIs. The results can be assessed by finding the correct nonfinancial metrics reliably predicting outcomes and financial performance. The process cannot be accomplished through intuition, raw judgement, gut feel, or salience. It requires in-depth analysis using advanced statistical techniques that can simultaneously analyze hundreds of KPIs and isolate the few most predictive of key outcomes.

10.6   Conclusion

Strategy planning is a vital contribution of CEOs and senior executives. Strategy planning should advance the interests of a company's customers, shareholders, employees, and other stakeholders. However, strategy planning as practiced by many companies does not deliver on its promise of creating shareholder value. This need not be the case. The process can be enabled to defeat the deleterious effects of strategy planning inhibitors, such as salience, staying put, intuitive leaps, use of mythical numbers, more-is-better thinking, and inward focus.

Enabling strategy requires senior executives to understand the frustrations their CEOs experience. And CEOs must ensure their direct reports embrace scientific analysis and statistically valid reasoning when making strategy decisions. In the end, the changes should increase the strategy planning quotient of a company's senior executives, CEOs, and the process itself.

Notes

1. Nisar, Tahir M. (2006), "Subjective performance measures in bonus payouts," *Performance Improvement*, 45(8), 34–40.
2. Mittal, Vikas, and Shrihari Sridhar (2020), "Customer based execution and strategy: Enhancing the relevance & utilization of B2B scholarship in the C-suite," *Industrial Marketing Management*, 88(July), 396–409.

Index

A

Accountability, 12, 21, 23, 27
Achieve more by doing less,
    131, 133–134
Acquisition target, 83
Adaptability, 70
Adaptive strategy, 66
Adhocracy, 65–77
Adhocratic strategy, 65–73, 77
Ambidexterity, 69
Analysis paralysis, 17–18

B

Benchmarking results, 171
Bias, 102, 107, 111, 114
Board member, 11
Branding, 156
Budget-based strategy, 43, 81–96
Business plan, 83

C

CEO perspective, 11–24
CEO survey, 31
Chain-link, 130, 131, 136, 138
Chief executive officer (CEO), 2, 4, 6,
    8, 9, 25–29, 31, 40, 43, 44

Chief financial officer (CFO), 82, 86, 91
Communication, 49, 56, 84, 90, 91
Confirmation bias, 102, 107
Coordination cost, 70, 71, 73, 77
Corporate budgeting, 81
Corporate culture, 48, 49
Corporate mission, 48
Corporate values, 48
Correlation, 29, 31–35, 37, 38,
    40, 42, 43
Counselor-in-chief, 159–161
Culture-based strategy, 47
Customer assessment, 150, 156
Customer focus, 149
Customer value, 16, 19–21, 23, 146,
    148–153, 155–157
Customer-value driver, 6
Custom-home builders, 144–148, 150,
    154, 155

D

Decision biases, 128
Decision-making, 9
Decision velocity, 70, 71
Decoupled measurement, 119–121
Diffuse accountability, 119–121
Discordant, 115–118

© The Author(s), under exclusive license to Springer Nature Switzerland AG 2021
V. Mittal, S. Sridhar, *Focus*, https://doi.org/10.1007/978-3-030-70720-0

E

Efficiency, 81, 83, 88, 89, 93–96
Emergent strategy, 1, 65
Employee engagement, 52
Employee motivation, 52, 53
Enablers, 127–140
Execution levers, 164, 169, 170
Executive alignment, 24
Executive perspective, 29
Experimentation, 65, 69, 77
Exploitation, 68, 69, 71, 77
Exploration, 68–71, 77

F

False associations, 105
Financial performance, 69, 72, 73
Financial planning, 29–31, 34, 35,
    37, 38, 43
Firefighter-in-chief, 159, 161
First-mover advantage, 72, 73
Focus, 127–129, 131–135, 138
Focus and sequence, 20–21

G

Give-get score, 132–134

H

Humility, 132, 139–140

I

Implementation tracking, 171
Implementer-in-chief, 159, 161, 162
Importance, 131–133, 135, 137, 138
Inertia, 114
Inhibitors, 99–121
Initial sales and bidding, 56, 57
Inputs, throughputs, and outputs,
    129–133, 137
Inspirational strategy, 47–62

Interdependence, 70
Internally focused strategy, 13, 16, 145
Intervening processes, 107
Intuitive leap, 103–110, 115–120
Inward-looking strategy, 14
Inwardly focused, 115–118

L

Linkage, 129–132, 137, 140
Loss aversion, 111

M

Machine learning, 135, 138
Margin expansion, 18
Marketing communication, 156
Mediating processes, 107
Mission statement, 48–62
Multiple determinants of
    outcomes, 106
Mythical numbers, 108–110,
    115, 118–120

N

New customer acquisition, 145, 157
No-defect installation, 149, 150, 152,
    153, 157
Not-to-do list, 134–135

O

Oil and gas, 56, 58, 59, 62
Ongoing service and support, 52,
    56–60, 95
Operational excellence, 81, 95
Oversimplified reality, 104

P

Planning fallacy, 113
Planning template, 136–137

Predictive KPIs, 171
Pricing and billing, 56, 58, 60, 91, 95
Prioritizing strategy areas, 169, 170
Private equity, 12, 22, 83, 85
Product and service quality, 56, 57,
    91, 92, 95
Product innovation, 73, 74
Project management, 56

R

Relative importance, 100, 102, 104,
    105, 113, 119–121
Research and development (R&D), 69,
    71–73, 75, 77
Return on investment (ROI), 72,
    73, 86–88
Return on strategy, 9

S

Safety, 56, 61, 91
Sales growth, 11, 13, 18–21, 23, 146,
    149, 151, 152
Salience, 100–103, 105, 115, 116, 119,
    120, 128, 130–133, 136, 138
Science-based strategy, 138
Self-assessment, 128
Service-support managers, 155
Small business, 65, 66
Social responsibility and
    sustainability, 56
Speed of installation, 149, 150, 152
Stability, 68, 69, 71, 72
Startup, 65, 66, 71

Statistical analysis, 100, 102, 106, 120,
    132, 138
Status-quo bias, 111
Staying put, 110–114
Strategic area, 96
Strategic plan, 1, 3
Strategy alignment, 27, 36, 39,
    40, 42, 43
Strategy area, 56–62
Strategy complexity, 113
Strategy consensus, 117, 118
Strategy dilemma, 145–149
Strategy execution, 27, 28, 66, 68, 75
Strategy goals, 37, 40
Strategy initiatives, 3, 18, 19
Strategy journey, 151
Strategy-leader-in-chief, 160, 162
Strategy map, 129–131, 133, 136,
    137, 140
Strategy plan, 25, 27, 29, 36–44
Strategy planning, 1–9, 11–44
Strategy planning framework,
    169–171
Strategy planning quotient,
    4–9, 159–172
Strategy retreat, 147–148

T

Technology, 73–76
10-K statement, 58

V

Vision, 47–62